AWAKENING THE MYSTIC

Adventures in Living From the Heart

NANCY LEE AND CECELIA KEENAN

Bloomington, IN

authorHOUSE

Milton Keynes, UK

AuthorHouse™
1663 Liberty Drive, Suite 200
Bloomington, IN 47403
www.authorhouse.com
Phone: 1-800-839-8640

AuthorHouse™ UK Ltd.
500 Avebury Boulevard
Central Milton Keynes, MK9 2BE
www.authorhouse.co.uk
Phone: 08001974150

This book is a work of non-fiction. Unless otherwise noted, the author and the publisher make no explicit guarantees as to the accuracy of the information contained in this book and in some cases, names of people and places have been altered to protect their privacy.

First published by AuthorHouse 7/27/2006

ISBN: 1-4259-2256-2 (sc)

Printed in the United States of America
Bloomington, Indiana

This book is printed on acid-free paper.

DEDICATION

We lovingly dedicate this book to our parents, Frances Ouida Giles Lee and James Jonathan Lee. We also bless our ancestors from the bloodlines of Lee, Giles, Arrant and Hart who hail from their beloved homelands of England, Ireland, Scotland and France. And we honor our Native American heritage, born of the Cherokee tribe, whose heart beats within us.

We thank our siblings, James, Michael and Kelly, for their willingness to share their gifts with us in this incarnation. And we honor our children, Katherine, Brent, Robert and Lee.

Special thanks also go to Tom Keenan, Cynthia Butler, Brian Colon, Laurel Lund and Dr. Mark Boyd, whose tireless efforts have helped create this printed work from countless hours of dictation, editing, transcription and design.

TABLE OF CONTENTS

Dedication v

Foreword..ix

NANCY'S PATH

Living In Both Worlds 3

Mirror Of Dorothy 13

Dreams Of Awakening..17

When Angels Come..22

Aspen Winter 25

Glastonbury Abbey..32

CECELIA'S PATH

On The Edge 37

Inter-Dimensional Artisans 47

Spiritual Magic..51

Visions Of The Garden..56

THE TEACHINGS

Introduction To The Teachings...61

The Ancient Ones 65

Beyond The Illlusion..75

Creating Your World 83

Expanding The Light..92

Lessons For The Soul..97

The Power Of Intention 104

The Open Heart 110

Returning Home 118

Your Spiritual Family 127

Twin Flame Sexualtiy 132

The Nature Of Perfection 141

Ascension: Becoming Your Future Self 145

Blessing 148

FOREWORD

Mystic: one who follows, advocates, or experiences the mystical; a belief in direct knowledge of God or ultimate reality as attainable through intuition or insight.

Our planet earth is in a spectacular phase of growth and change. We, as a species, stand at the threshold of evolution and responsibility for choosing whether we will move forward in love, compassion, and awareness; or if we will remain stuck in the mire that we were born into – never finding freedom's door. In this exciting and pivotal time of evolutionary awakening, we have chosen to participate in raising the frequency of light to help expand the consciousness of humanity. This expansion must come from the heart and soul of each individual as we emerge as universal beings. It must ultimately lead to an understanding of our connection to God and to each other.

Throughout the entire universe all eyes are on us, watching and waiting to see how we will handle these crucial decisions. Will we continue down that dark path of annihilation and destroy our world, or will we grow as kindred spirits who honor and respect each other as mutual custodians of this planet?

A host of dedicated spirit friends watch lovingly as they purposefully seek to guide us to the truth of our ultimate reality with God. In opening to the assistance of this unseen, vast universal knowledge, we learn to open to the greater truth within that connects us to all things. We further find that in accepting the divinity of our own Soul, and that of all others, we will find our way Home.

Eventually we will not need the interpretation of guides or spirit friends, for our own connection to Spirit becomes clear and strong. But we come to understand our promptings from spirit as well as we understand our best friend's warning or congratulation. As we escalate up the rungs of ascension, we will finally operate fully as our own Higher Selves, that larger part of us that is directly connected to Creator. But along the way we have found the input of our spirit friends and guides to be extremely helpful. They have helped us to awaken the limitless spiritual nature of our existence, and to comfort and console when we have lost our footing along the way.

People from all walks of life are beginning to recognize themselves as greater than they once seemed, and are viewing their world with a spiritual maturity unknown to the vast majority in previous generations. There is a great curiosity and inspiration to become more, yet to find the simplicity inherent in all genius. Old belief systems of judgment and separation are losing ground as we embrace a more compassionate way of relating to the world. And in this world of duality we learn to recognize the darkness and the light as both sides of the same coin, and see that darkness is the absence of light.

Self-awareness is replacing blind acceptance of the old programs, and intuition is becoming the new yardstick in this emerging paradigm, as the mystical awakens within. Silently, through telepathy, we radiate our frequency to those of like mind, and to those with whom we have unfinished business. Our drama plays out on an "as needed" basis, and we receive blessings of grace when our gratitude precedes our knowledge. Trust, faith and surrender open the pathway through the woods of our misunderstanding. We recognize "accidents" and "coincidences" are synchronized through our magnetic fields.

As sisters, we – Nancy Lee and Cecelia Keenan – have shared this remarkable journey together. We learned from an early age about keeping secrets, and assuming acceptable behaviors required in polite society. Growing up in the Deep South's Gulf Coast in the 1950's, we attended a Christian fundamentalist school until 'junior high', as it was then called. Even before the first grade, we had already been taught the shame, blame and guilt of 'original sin'.

In our spiritual journey from the darkness of judgment into the light of self-acceptance, we learned to listen to the Spirit that lives within and to hear the profound and loving messages from our Spirit Guides and Friends, often through meditations and prayers. This process deepened our mystical natures as we learned to follow our hearts.

Psychic: the ability to access beyond the five senses

Even though our conservative Christian upbringing frowned on anything psychic or cosmic in nature, we were both gifted children. Older sister Cecelia was wise beyond her years – precocious, outspoken, and fiery. I was clairvoyant from childhood and could see through the world's lies and hypocrisies. I held my knowledge silently inside to maintain peace, until I became older. That is when diplomacy allowed subjects to be discussed that were formerly unmentionable. My sister was born brunette, and I, blonde. Our personalities seemed as different as night and day. Born eighteen months apart, we have traveled our spiritual paths together; being both a support system for each other's expanding consciousness, and a repository for the secrets we could share with no one else.

Our highly competitive relationship was a battlefield on which many family dramas were played out. Day-and-night sisters, one of us took on the attributes of our mother and the other adapted the characteristics of our father as unhealed family issues came up for review and release. To complicate matters, we switched parental roles, back and forth, as our unconscious minds deemed necessary, to broaden our perspective. While participating in our family's healing process through our own unresolved issues, we learned that all healing is self-healing. What we do for ourselves, we do for the other; and for the other, ourselves. It is our own desire and intention to heal that brings the forgiveness that allows us the independence and freedom to proceed.

Giving ourselves permission to trust the spiritual guidance we have received allowed us to make many difficult decisions in our lives. This has not been a necessarily easy or comfortable path, and we have not always been led to places we consciously chose to visit. But it is the very trusting and surrendering that has moved us along on our paths. At times it felt as if we jumped out of the frying pan into the fire, only to be blessed with coming back into the light again. It was in these moments of grace that we learned to accept what *is* as perfection for the growth potential it offered.

The process of creating these chapters was a personal growth experience in and of itself. We found ourselves living the issues discussed within the context of each chapter. There were days when we found ourselves looking at each other in absolute wonder. A profound respect and a deepening love grew from the vestiges of former childhood competition.

This book is our offering for peace, love, consciousness, inspiration and hope. If these lofty goals reach any part of the reader's imagination, we encourage you to choose with courage what you wish to create in this world. We are all here to heal our hearts and to evolve our Souls. Whether our mission is of obvious global significance, or is extremely personal, it encompasses learning to honor and interpret the language of your Soul. It is only by learning to listen within and by following that which expands our hearts, that we awaken our mystical connection back to Source. In this way we evolve our personal sovereignty.

We are all works in process. Sometimes we find ourselves in the 'one – step forward, two- steps back' mode of spiritual awakening. And it is in the times when things seem not to be moving at all that some of our most profound integration is occurring. Be gentle with yourselves, and know that as children of God it is your birthright to experience life with as much joy, peace, and grace as you can muster. We are all here on a temporary pass, so make the most of the precious time and people you are blessed with in your lives.

It is our hope that you will find renewed faith and courage in these personal stories and spiritual messages. May they bring you the joy that comes from jumping into the stream of life with both feet and wading through its waters with grace!

Nancy Lee and Cecelia Keenan, 2006

PART I

NANCY'S PATH

Chapter One

LIVING IN BOTH WORLDS

You never know when or how the Angels will come.
—Nancy Lee

As a young child, I remember walking in the crisp autumn air, balancing atop concrete walls, looking down at the colored leaves on the ground and feeling a connection to the earth that invigorated me. All around me were vivid impressions of life, the magnificence of creation. I felt one with all things. Life belonged to Spirit—and it belonged to me.

But this was when I could still *see*, when I could still accept without question the beauty and majesty of Creator's world. This was before I felt forced by society to shut down my senses, to become cut off from my connection to Creator.

The fairies and Soul Friends no one else could see used to come to me in those times, much as they would with any child blessed with such openness—aware of the expanded gifts we bring to this earth plane. Like most children, I believed life was magical and without fear.

Such magic happened one day early in my childhood when, sitting with my mother in our home in Alabama, I looked across an open field and "saw" an encampment of nomadic Indians. There were warriors returning from the hunt, elderly women mending fur clothing, younger women talking over huge pots they were stirring, children laughing as they played with sticks. It was as though I were one of them, hearing what they were saying and feeling. As the visions drew closer, my feelings of connection became stronger. I felt as if I was returning home.

I turned to my Mother and told her what I was "seeing." Her look of confusion and worry stunned me and made me think there must be something wrong with my mind. At that moment, I knew this kind of information was never to be shared with others who could not see.

From the tender age of four, my siblings and I attended a fundamentalist Christian school that taught we were all born lost. It instilled in us a feeling that we were all very bad people. We were reminded daily that God would punish us for our sins and send us to Hell to burn for eternity if we offended Him in any way. It was in this atmosphere of fear that I became confused early on. I did not understand what was wrong with me, but some very powerful adults seemed to believe I was a sinner. I pretended to agree, but it was the beginning of my shutdown, my suppression of Self.

Our early years have a compelling influence on us. One of the most significant events of my early years occurred in the summer of 1954 when my sister Cecelia, age five, and I, age three, were making "medicine." We had concocted a remedy of Pepto Bismol and Prell, and we wanted to take it across the street to an elderly lady who not only welcomed us but also purchased our "remedies" for a nickel or a dime. As we began to cross the street, we walked with purpose. But suddenly, as we stood at the curb, a large, two-toned, green car swung around the corner. The next thing I knew, Cecelia was being dragged under the car down the block.

Standing only inches from her, I was miraculously unharmed. An Angel had grabbed me off the street. The Angel wore the body of a crippled man balancing on crutches, wearing braces from the waist down. Although he seemed ancient, he appeared from nowhere in an instant to save me. He was my first experience with an Angel.

After the accident, as Cecelia waited for the "white emergency people" to take her to the hospital, I remember entering my parent's room only to see Cecelia lying on the bed, bloodied and in great pain. I felt that my stomach had been ripped out, along with my heart. I felt totally alone, with no one to hold me or to explain what was happening.

Cecelia spent two months confined to her hospital bed with a broken leg, broken jaw and numerous other injuries. The school principal that had been the driver of the car was her most frequent visitor, bringing so many gifts that they filled her room to overflowing, so she shared them with children in the other wards.

Meanwhile, the doctors told our parents that Cecelia would most likely always walk with a limp, if she recovered at all. Thankfully, they were wrong. Instead, she became the fastest runner, the quickest swimmer and the toughest kid in the neighborhood!

During that time, it was difficult being apart. I was too young to visit her at the hospital. But sometimes—while waiting in the car in the parking lot, many stories below, with our father—Cecelia would wave to me from the window. Still, those days were sad and lonely. The accident changed our lives forever; the joy and freedom of early childhood were stolen from us that day.

The accident also brought about other changes. I missed not going to ballet class anymore, and I missed Cecelia. Suddenly, our family life revolved around her healing. I began experiencing issues around self-esteem and learned not to ask for what I needed.

We have since learned that on a Soul level, the accident was Cecelia's bold attempt to leave the planet. Her Soul had been uncomfortable in her body, and she had a restless spirit. Little did anyone know about the Angel that assisted Cecelia in staying on the earth plane or my guilt about the fact that she was injured and I was safe.

Our relationship has been the catalyst for so many things, including my early spiritual growth. When I resisted using my psychic gifts or trusting my own guidance in order to fit in, to be socially acceptable, it was Cecelia who urged me to respect my gifts.

This affected my life positively because, despite my inner turmoil, I did very well blending in. During my freshman year in high school, I was voted Most Popular. Eventually, I was elected cheerleader, Class Favorite and Homecoming Queen. I was also president of our local store's Teen Board and a teen model. Still, few of my friends knew the real me.

When we try to suppress who we are and what we feel, we often use physical or social means. Throughout my early adulthood, I tried all manner of fitting-in techniques—from marrying early because it was "the thing to do" to using alcohol and later experimenting with mild recreational drugs as a way of placating unwanted emotions.

During the Viet Nam era of the 1960s and 1970s, the societal lies we believed were that we were supposed to be sexually liberated —"love the one you're with"—that we were going to die young, that we were privy to the secret meaning of the universe and that we were living in an era of personal freedom.

Even though I wanted to fit into the world our society taught us was real, my inner voice always pulled me back to my own center, my Soul. This spiritual badminton went on for years. Any disappointments I felt manifested themselves in pain in my abdomen or my heart. Deep inside, I may have known I was living a lie, but I refused to believe it. Instead, I shut down emotionally and mentally, something that continued until my body eventually manifested intestinal blockages, anorexia and colitis.

Because of this, I found myself in the most severe physical trauma. By the fall of 1994, I became quite ill from ulcerative colitis. Loss of blood left me too weak to even lift the telephone. Having been to my local hospital in Fort Collins, Colorado, twice, to no avail, I was sent to a nearby hospital in Loveland, Colorado, for further tests.

The day before my 6:00 a.m. check-in, Cecelia once again prodded me on. She rushed into my home, saying, "I know there is a message for you. You have to connect and get the message."

Although I felt almost too ill to connect, I tried. Instantly, a voice rushed through me saying, "We know you have decided to leave the earth plane. If you will stay here and do this work, we will help you."

I had not realized how gravely ill I was because I had gotten so good at masking my feelings. But I was dying. Humbled, I began to reflect on my life. How had it come to this? I was only 40-something. I had given birth to two wonderful children who were just beginning their journeys into adulthood, and they needed me. My love for my children had always given me the strength to endure life's disappointments, but the painful struggle of this life had left me empty and tired. Having once thought death might be a blessing, I now thought, "Wait a minute. I have not done what I came here to do. I can't leave now!" I didn't want to die.

I knew that there was a special reason for my presence in this lifetime and that I would have to find the courage to find it. I couldn't imagine how to live my Inner Spirit in the outer world, but I knew I must in order to continue this journey. Even if it meant ridicule, even if no one else accepted me for who I was, I wanted to live—to express who I came here to be. I wanted to help others—if it wasn't too late. In that moment, the power we have to create our own reality was stunningly clear.

Professionally, I had been in the advertising and computer industries and had worked as a pharmaceutical representative immediately after college. In these arenas I became very successful using my mind in a "man's world." I learned to mask my true feelings in order to fit in and excel at their game. I raised my children on commissions earned in these fields but lost bits of my Soul as I became the masculine version of myself rather than the embodiment of wholeness.

In our search for balance, the pendulum often swings to opposite ends of the spectrum—from how to embody the essence of our Soul in a world of matter to how to honor our true Self while accomplishing tasks in the outer world. I did not make the rules of **the outer world,** but, suddenly, it seemed I had let the battle for Self go on for too long.

Through the magical synchronicity of the universe, on the evening before I was to return to the hospital for additional tests, my front doorbell rang and before me stood an earthly "angel"—my friend Irving Shepherd, DO, a chiropractor from Fairhope, Alabama, who was traveling in Colorado. I invited him in, and we talked for hours. Although he did not know about my illness, he intuited that something was amiss. So he pulled out his collection of crystals and other healing tools and worked on my energy field to release issues around self worth. Then, we continued talking through the night about what beliefs were blocking my will to live. As it became clear, the Absolute Truth resonating within was this prayer to Creator.

Dear God,
I am not ready to join You
unless it is Your will that I do so at
this time.
I do not want to die; too many things
are left undone.
I will stay here and do Your work
willingly
if there is still time.
Help me do what I've come here to do.
Please show me what that is.
I will no longer resist the essence of
who I am,
The gift that You have given me is
myself.
I am humbled in the recognition of
this truth.
Find me worthy to do Your work.
I will comply.
Thank You, God.
Amen.

Cecelia and Irving drove me to the hospital the next morning and waited for me while I underwent tests. During the entire procedure, I had a unique sense of destiny. I wasn't frightened, but I wanted to pass these tests more than anything I had ever wanted in my life. I realized how cut off I had been from my own spiritual nature, and I wanted to have access to the full expression of my Soul. For the first time since childhood, I was aware that the gift of life and my own unique expression of that life was my gift back to humanity.

I prayed again. When you pray from the depth of your soul, your prayers are answered. Mine were. The miracle that occurred next will stay with me forever. The diagnosis: Clean Bill of Health. The doctors found no tumors, no bleeding and no colitis—just the signs of a healthy body. They were puzzled that my condition did not match my diagnosis. I was not.

Cecelia, Irving and I celebrated my medical miracle by heading to the nearest restaurant for fried catfish, something I'd been craving. On the way, Irving related another magical piece of the story. That morning, he had carried healing, diamond-cut amethysts in his pocket. He told me that while I was being examined, the amethysts began to get hot. The longer I was in the examination room, the hotter the crystals got. Midway through the procedure, the stones were so hot he couldn't touch them. When the procedure was over, unbeknownst to him, they cooled down completely—all of which Cecelia witnessed.

I excitedly asked to see the crystals, but when Irving reached into his pocket, the healing stones had disappeared—vanished from the planet. What had reappeared, however, was my health. I had been granted a new lease on life, and I wanted to make the best of it.

Prior to this event, I did psychic readings for friends, family and others who asked for my help. But even when I made it clear to them that I didn't want to do them anymore, Cecelia persuaded me to at least "go into connection" for her. When I did, information appeared to me visually. I "saw" pictures, symbols, scenes, expanding and contracting energies, words and phrases. An intuitive sense, a *knowing*, came over me and chills ran up my spine.

Our paternal grandmother had this same sense of knowing. She had always been recognized for her psychic abilities, but they were not discussed in polite Southern society. Her son, our father, was also extremely psychically gifted. I remember how he loved to go to the shopping mall, sit on a bench and focus on the arm of a passerby until the person scratched or swatted it. It was great fun!

After my miraculous recovery, I still had no desire to come out of the clairvoyant closet. I didn't want my clients to question the source of my awareness. I wanted them to think it came from my vocational or educational background. But my Soul knew I didn't want to deceive or manipulate anyone with those earth-plane values.

That's when I chose to talk openly about my spiritual life. I explained to many members of my family, friends and clients that when I close my eyes and ask for clarity, vision and illumination, I receive pictures, symbols, words or energies of revelation. They appear in a form relevant only to the person asking the question, whether it be myself or a client. In fact, it is a true test of my own faith to share what I receive, even when it makes no sense to me.

My readings changed form over the years, becoming easier for me to understand. I became comfortable trusting the information I received and allowing my own Higher Self to speak.

Once I was open and frank about my gift with those who showed interest, I began to host personal evening and weekend sessions, make radio appearances, become a full-time spiritual/clairvoyant consultant and create my own radio show about spiritual and metaphysical topics. I felt joy in openly sharing my gift to help others. The more I became comfortable with this, the more my heart opened and the more solidly my health returned. I had been given another chance at life, and I was now on the path of my own Higher Self—here to serve, to manifest and to give others the courage to do the same.

When I conceived my radio program, "Lights On with Nancy Lee"—which focuses on how to turn on our Inner light and listen to the Spirit within—the time from conception to realization was only two weeks. I was terrified! I knew much about radio advertising and sales but nothing about actual broadcasting. As with most people, I had avoided public speaking—one of people's top fears, along with death and divorce. But from my first moment on the air, everything unfolded as it should. Things sometimes happened with grace and ease. Other times, they occurred in a two-steps-forward, one-step-back manner. But everything is easier when it comes as part of the Divine plan. The blessings of listening to Spirit, following guidance and being a vessel to help expand Spirit in others have been enormous.

The incredible people who have been guests on my radio show have graced my life—and the lives of others. Some of the most gifted thinkers and the bravest souls on the planet have helped bring forth the message of change, courage, hope and empowerment so we all may become the most highly expanded versions of ourselves. My guests have included traditional medical doctors, homeopathic physicians, natural healers, psychics, psychologists and authors of self-help, spiritual, metaphysical and health books. Also gracing the show's airwaves are best-selling authors Neale Donald Walsch, Marianne Williamson, Dr. Doreen Virtue, Gregg Braden and Lee Carroll, as well as many currently unknown people who have precious gifts to share.

The blessings that have come into my life since allowing my Essential Self to come forward are profound. When Spirit flows freely through us and we honor the feelings in our hearts, we feel the richness of being truly alive in the present moment.

Chapter Two

MIRROR OF DOROTHY

Dorothy Giles, my mother's younger sister, died on Thanksgiving Day, 1949. At the young age of 17, she quietly slipped to the other side after having gone to her room for a short nap before Thanksgiving dinner. When my mother went to wake her, she found her cold and lifeless body sitting upright, at ease against the bed's headboard, as if she had simply dozed off.

Dorothy's mother, our grandmother Lula Giles, was devastated. Her grief was intensified by the fact that Dorothy had only been a baby when Lula's husband, had died many years before from a heart attack while helping a local schoolteacher change a flat tire.

Further intensifying Grandmother Lula's grief was discovering that Dorothy had died for naught. For six weeks prior to her death, she had been using a drug-store purchased skin-cream product widely used for acne. It was later found that the product appeared to have poisoned her.

After the county coroner ruled Dorothy's cause of death as poison, interesting events occurred. First, the suspected skin cream disappeared from the drug store shelves. The hospital records, along with her autopsy report, vanished. And, strangely, when later asked, no one could remember the circumstances that may have led to her death—the company that manufactured the skin cream had hushed up the cause.

It was soon discovered that others had died under similar circumstances, but there was no evidence to support the suspicion. It was as if Dorothy had not died that Thanksgiving Day.

But she had. Grandmother Lula told me years later, tears in her eyes, that there is no pain in life equal to that of losing a child. She had outlived four husbands, survived the burning of her home and overcome countless obstacles in her long life, but she never got over losing Dorothy.

Unbeknownst to me, I helped keep memories of Dorothy alive. From my earliest years, my mother's family members would say: "You look like Dorothy." "You walk like Dorothy." "You have the same mannerisms as Dorothy." "Your legs are shaped like Dorothy's." "My goodness, don't you smile just like Dorothy?"

There were other similarities. When I gazed at Dorothy's photo, I could see myself; I didn't look like my mother or my father, but I had an uncanny resemblance to Dorothy. Perhaps Dorothy's death at age 17 is also the reason I never thought I would live past that age.

I don't think these are mere coincidences. Six different psychics have since told me that at the age of four I was a walk-in, a Soul that takes over the body of another Soul in order to help the first Soul complete their earthly destiny. Apparently, the Soul of my youngest brother, Michael, held my body for me while my own Soul was off completing other tasks in order to reincarnate. Once I took over my body, Michael was born back into my genealogical family two years later. I don't know if the story is true, but I do believe that Soul-shifting and walk-in experiences are possible, that our Souls are free to come and go and be born and reborn, again and again.

Another example of a Soul leaving its original body, yet living on, is my son Brent. He died in my arms at the age of nineteen months. He had been a normal, healthy child with boundless energy right up until the night before his passing. The next day, he woke up pale and in great discomfort, so I took him to the doctor's office—three times. Twice, the physicians told me he had a sore throat, sending him home with throat spray and baby Tylenol. But he continued to grow worse throughout the day. During the third visit, a female doctor came toward us with her hand held up, as if to silence us so she could hear something.

Realizing something was seriously wrong with my baby, she said, "You must not let your baby know anything is wrong, but if we don't get him to the emergency room right away, we will lose him."

At that, I went numb, babbling about finding my car keys, but the doctor offered to drive us to the hospital. I sat in the passenger seat, rocking my ailing child who was starting to turn blue. He pushed weakly against me. Suddenly, his movements stopped, his head rolled back on my arm and his eyes froze in place. No sound escaped his lips. No breath moved in or out of his body. Pleading for my son's life, I screamed at God, which caused the doctor to skid onto the median.

Miraculously, my baby son suddenly began to moan. At that, the doctor immediately restarted the car and raced for the hospital. When we got to the emergency room, a group of other doctors were waiting to take him out of my arms.

Brent was diagnosed with a rare condition that very few physicians are aware of, let alone know its source or its prevention: epiglottitis—a state in which the epiglottis swells shut, literally suffocating the bearer to death. Over the next three weeks, Brent went through a series of tracheotomies to alleviate the condition. But we never knew if he would make it through the next surgery. In the meantime, I stayed by his side, day and night, sleeping on a small cot in the intensive care unit, praying myself to sleep.

Miraculously, Brent recovered. But he was never again the same child—not better or worse, just different. At first, I thought his personality had changed because he had been through such trauma. But it was more than that. A mother knows her child, and this was not the same child I had known as Brent. Everything about him changed—from his walk to the shape of his body. He had been his father's son prior to the incident, all rough and tumble. Suddenly, he was my son, much like my side of the family—more reflective and less rambunctious.

As if to underscore my feeling that Brent's Soul had vacated his body for another's, in grade school Brent would introduce me to his friends by saying, "I just wanted you to meet my daughter, Nancy." And often, during periods of confusion or disappointment, he would say to me, "You know that I am only here for you because you wouldn't let me leave."

Chapter Three

DREAMS OF AWAKENING

It is easy to dismiss what happens in dreamtime in favor of waking reality. In fact, it is not unusual to have no memory of your dreams at all. But as we become more conscious of those dreams, they become important in helping us understand who we are and what we need.

Dreams can be precognitive, foretelling future events. Dreams can be cognitive, alerting us to a dramatic event as it occurs. Dreams can be post-cognitive, educating us about our past lifetimes, other incarnations. Or dreams can be other-dimensionally cognitive, bringing us messages from the Angels.

Dreams can also be healing. loved ones may appear, offering messages of hope, comfort or farewell—particularly if those messages were not possible to send on the physical plane.

When a dream occurs repeatedly, it is a sign that something needs our attention. Even if the dream is not the same but the *theme* is the same, it requires attention. It may give us insight into unexplained fears or phobias, unearth subconscious desires, assist in solving problems or point us in new directions. Dreams may, indeed, have many purposes, but they are always for the one who dreams.

Some philosophies hold that when we sleep, our Souls travel into the Astral plane and beyond. Here, we experience levels of Consciousness not possible in our dense earth plane. We must travel beyond the earthly veil of ignorance of All There Is in order to go into the void and extract the messages of Spirit.

Some of my more meaningful dreams follow, all of which helped me along Life's path.

Dream No. 1

It was the early autumn of 1763 in the hills of Tennessee, and I was running for my life! An unknown Native American was chasing me through the woods. I kept looking back, again and again, to determine how far away he was, when I stumbled, gasping for breath. My pursuer ran even faster, as if no branches tore at his face, no thorns wrapped his legs.

The skirt of my long, brown cotton dress, with its prim white collar, rustled around my ankles, nearly tripping me as I ran.

I was 17 years old. My family had moved on without me days ago when they thought I was lost, and I was completely alone and frightened in those woods. I felt a sense of frantic doom as I was running, as though I was in a dream within a dream

Panting, I finally reached a clearing. I felt relief for a brief moment until I realized I was standing at the edge of a cliff. But my pursuer continued running toward me—his eyes filled with malice, his jaw twisted in a grimace, his hands clawing at the air.

In my fear, I jumped off the cliff and died.

This dream repeated itself for months. It started the same year I met and fell in love with a man. The dreams continued until we married and moved to the woods of Tennessee several years later. I did not realize the significance of the dream until midway through my marriage.

Like anyone in love, I knew my marriage would be a wonderful one! I was proud of my husband, who everyone considered amazing. He was successful in the banking industry and held many impressive positions in the public service arena. No one suspected he was a tyrant at home and that I was his virtual prisoner.

My husband was opposed to any expression of my spiritual awareness, past-life recall, metaphysical interest and ability to "see" his activities even when he was absent—not a plus for an unfaithful spouse. His extracurricular activities would spring into my consciousness regardless of where or when they would happen.

The true me, who had struggled so hard to come out of the spiritual closet, was someone I barely recognized anymore. As I had done in my youth, I shut down my natural expression to maintain peace in the household. But it was rendering me more and more lifeless.

I knew the pain of leaving the relationship would be intense, but the lesson learned from the experience was noble: When we betray ourselves, as I did when I failed to heed the meaning of my dream, someone else enters our lives to betray us too. What we experience outside ourselves is what we experience inside, much like looking into a mirror. If we honor ourselves, others will honor us. Being true to ourselves is very serious soul business; to paraphrase William Shakespeare in Hamlet: When you are true to yourself, you cannot be false to any man.

Dream No. 2

Before leaving Tennessee, I started seeing a man's face in my dreams, a unique face I had never seen before. The man had light eyes and full lips tucked inside a close-cropped beard. He seemed curious about me. He appeared night after night, floating up in front of me, looking into my face and then drifting away.

This dream was strangely comforting in the midst of the changes occurring in my marital life. I had discovered bugging devices in my home and undeniable proof that every phone call, made or received, was being recorded. As a result, I went to bed every night with knots in my stomach, sleeping in the fetal position for protection, my estranged husband sleeping only inches away.

With the help of my brother, Jim, and my lawyer, I finally left my home and my marriage and moved back to Mobile, Alabama.

Two weeks after arriving in Mobile, my divorce papers signed, I accepted a job with Entre' Computer Center selling IBM software for the medical and legal fields. Several weeks into the job, I made an appointment to have my employee photo taken. But when the photographer greeted me at the door, I nearly fainted. That face—it was the face from my dreams! Standing in front of me, in the flesh, was the exact same face that had appeared to me in Tennessee.

The name behind the face was Alan, a photographer from New York City who had taken a detour to the South. Our connection was instantaneous. I was intrigued with him immediately because of our introduction in my dreams, and he was interested in me for his own reasons. We became close friends, but as much as I tried to remain just friends, I failed. He wanted to get married; yet I knew I still had tremendous healing and processing to go through before I could contemplate a serious commitment.

No matter. During this healing process, it was Alan who helped me pick up the shattered pieces of my life. I think that is what made me fall in love with him. But I later learned that in a past life together, he had felt emasculated by me and feared the same again in this lifetime.

Just as Alan is my Soul connection from another lifetime, so are many of our fellow journeyers on this earth plane. Souls enter our lives for many reasons—most are simply companions along the way, while others are here to teach us valuable lessons or learn from us. Some Soul Friends spark our growth by leaving our lives rather than by staying. Some are here to nurture us through the most difficult times—others are here to celebrate our success, our beauty, and our growth.

Once we had shared our gifts with each other, Alan and I parted. To bring a little joy back into my life, I planned a trip to Birmingham, Alabama, to attend a ballet performance with Cecelia and my sister-in-law, Julie—a decision that provided me another gift beyond my imagination.

The evening following the ballet, as the three of us headed back to the Gulf Coast south on I-65, we noticed some smoky white clouds through the open sunroof of Cecelia's Volvo. They came together in a perfectly formed cross against a deep, black sky. All the stars behind it had vanished into the dark night, and only one star remained—shining brightly at the intersection of the cross. Though interstate traffic had been heavy, suddenly there were no other cars on the road. Here we were, completely alone on an empty highway, watching a giant cross in the sky overhead that seemed to guide us down the highway.

After several minutes, the cross disappeared, jolting us back into the "real world"— horns honking and engines roaring down the highway. But we felt an uncanny sense of being a part of something grand, as though a magician's hand had painted the sky exclusively for us, sending an encoded signal we did not yet understand. It gave me hope for the life to come.

Chapter Four

WHEN ANGELS COME

After returning to the Gulf Coast in the late 1980s, I traveled farther down my spiritual path while my children and I were happily ensconced in a lovely patio home. It was here that I had one of the most incredible experiences in my life.

Out of a sound sleep one evening, I was jarred awake by a commotion. Someone was trying to break into our home! I was terrified knowing that my children, Katherine and Brent, were sleeping in bedrooms close to the main entryway.

I bolted out of bed and, in seconds, rounded the door to the living room, where I froze in place. Instead of a human intruder, I was stunned to see several human-size Angelic Beings of light. Gathered in a semi-circle around the rounded glass patio enclosure outside, there were eight entities—light green in color—that seemed to float down from the sky, softly touching the ground. Then, a large male entity dressed in a square-shaped head cap floated down. His back faced me, and his arms extended outward like bird wings from beneath his cape. Clearly the leader of the group, he slowly turned his head toward me with the biggest smile spread across his face. I felt protected, and unconditional love flowed straight into my heart.

I will never forget that Angel's face, one that I would one day encounter in human form. When I did, I laughed uncontrollably but dared not explain my odd behavior. How can you explain something like this to a "stranger?" The stranger's name was Paul, and as our friendship developed, I gladly shared with him that his face was the same face as the Captain of the Angels who had protected my children and me from harm.

When I saw the angels standing guard in my living room, I knew that whoever or whatever had tried to threaten my family had departed. As I returned to bed, I saw outside a row of tiny, fairy-like, crystal blue Angels circling the entire household. Their light energy created an aura of protection. I knew then that my home and family were safe.

Thank you, dear God.

Thank you Spirit of Grace,

protection and eternal love.

Thank you for taking care of my children.

Even in my unconscious state,

sleeping unaware,

You have been ever watchful,

keeping us safe from harm.

I feel completely loved in more ways

than I could ever imagine.

Amen.

You really never know when, or in what form, an Angel will appear. It may appear as a green or blue etheric form or as a great white orb of light. It may come in the form of an animal. It may appear as sparkling flashes of light that dance between you and another. Or,

It may appear in the form of a human—perhaps as a broken-down, crippled man who saves you from an out-of-control car or as an incredibly gleeful Bo Jangles-style musician.

One stormy day shortly after the break-in incident, when I was feeling slightly blue, just such an Angel appeared to me.

Cecelia and I had driven to a local bookstore to pick up a highly touted new book on metaphysics. It was raining so hard that rainwater threatened to wash over the curbing, and we could barely see anything ahead of us through the windshield. When we arrived at the bookstore, I waited in the car while Cecelia ran inside to buy the book. As I was sitting in the front seat, looking at nothing in particular, I was suddenly startled by a face that seemed to zoom up in front of the car window. The face was that of a young black man whose smile stretched all the way across his plump cheeks—a smile that melted my heart. As I watched, the young man began to dance Bo Jangles-style, a beautiful soft-shoe number. He danced and twirled with abandon around puddles of rainwater. But he never looked wet, nor did he slip in the water. And then, just as instantly as he appeared, he vanished before my eyes.

Was he an Angel? I think so. He left me with an incredible feeling of joy that stays with me still. He warmed my life with *his* love of life and his unbridled freedom of movement.

Chapter Five

ASPEN WINTER

The Aspen tree is a part of a unified grove, attached by its root system under the earth, making it one of the largest organisms on this planet. The Aspens seem to stand individually, but underneath is their connection through the largest of all root systems.

—Nancy Lee

Through a series of adversities and financial reversals, Cecelia and her husband had closed their once-successful interior design business, filed bankruptcy and sought opportunities elsewhere. After much searching, her husband accepted a manufacturer's representative position based in Fort Collins, Colorado, where his territories included Colorado and Wyoming.

I helped them move to their new home in Colorado, but I wasn't impressed with the area. I have since changed my mind.

When my mother and I visited Cecelia and her husband a year later, we had an incredible experience on the second day of our visit, September 9, 1990. We were driving through Estes Park, winding our way through beautiful Aspen groves and listening to the radio, singing along with Mariah Carey's "Vision of Love" and the Neville Brothers' "Fearless"—expansive, positive music.

During this drive, I felt a change in my vibration. I felt like I could reach out and touch the trees, taking their energy into my body. What began as a feeling became a buzzing that culminated with a deep knowing, a profound Truth, within. I heard, "You are moving here. This is your new home." Tears poured from my eyes. This is not what I had planned for my life, but I did not question it. I knew at some level that it was true.

Knowing it was true didn't help. I lived in Mobile, where at this time I was a successful headhunter for a local employment-recruiting firm. My two children were entrenched in school and social activities. I was in a loving relationship and enjoying many spiritual activities. My friends and family spent many weekends on the white, sandy beaches of Destin, Florida, with younger sister Kelly, a bright, vibrant, fun-loving Leo. Life felt beautifully balanced. I felt young, slim, tan and spiritually savvy—quite a feat for a woman about to turn 40. I was enjoying my life in Mobile, but I recognized that it was about to end.

After our visit, Mother and I flew home, and I immediately quit my job without giving notice. I then turned around and drove straight back to Colorado to find a job. Although two weeks later I still hadn't found employment—I didn't realize how difficult that might be, as even PhD's in Colorado were working as dishwashers and janitors just to be in the area!—I returned to Mobile to collect my son and gather what suitcases we could fit into our car and return to Colorado.

My friends in Mobile didn't approve of my change in lifestyle, however. They couldn't understand how a single mother of two children could pick up and leave for parts unknown without assurance of a job. Rumors about me in Mobile were rife—I had had a nervous breakdown, I was having a mid-life crisis, I was living in a van in the woods with a musician. But they were simply rumors, and none of them mattered. I knew I was doing what was right for my family and me, even though Brent, then 13 years old, would be angry about it for a long time.

Katherine, my eldest child, remained in Mobile to attend the University of South Alabama. A year later, however, her frequent visits to Colorado spurred her to move to my new home state to attend Colorado State University in Fort Collins.

Two weeks after moving to Colorado, I found a job with a local computer company.

That's when fortuitous events began to occur. I found myself working with a woman who loved to enter radio-station contests. When she won a free lunch for our entire company at a local restaurant, hosted by the station's deejays, one of the hosting deejays tried to recruit me for an ad sales position. Though flattered, I didn't pursue it.

Then I met another person who encouraged me to look into a career in radio communication, and the rest is history.

Contrary to the positive things that were happening in my life, negative things were also beginning to occur. Within six months, my father's second wife, Carolyn, who was five years younger than me, died suddenly and inexplicably on the operating table. My father was distraught. Now solely responsible for the care of the couple's five-year-old daughter and a teenage daughter from Carolyn's former marriage, he became depressed.

On New Year's Eve, six months after Carolyn's death, my father suffered a stroke. When it happened, I had been driving with a friend to Mesa Verde, Colorado, to see the Anasazi ruins. During the drive, I felt an incredible urge to call home. I tried repeatedly, but the phone lines were busy, and I couldn't get through until late that night. When I did get through, Mother answered the phone, and I knew immediately something was wrong. She told me that Dad had been found unconscious on the floor at his home due to a serious stroke and had been taken to the hospital. She urged Cecelia and me to come home quickly, which we did.

At the hospital, we sat by daddy's bed, but it was clear to us that he had already left his body. Over the next several days, we communicated telepathically. We shed many tears, but we also knew that he had wanted to leave for a long time. On January 13, 1991, two weeks after Cecelia and I had returned to Colorado, he died.

He was only 64 years of age at his death, but I think he had ultimately found this life to be a burden. The only male child and the youngest of five children in his family—he had four sisters who were as much as 12 to 22 years older when he was born—my father essentially grew up with five "mothers" who spoiled him. The result was a charming, artistic and musical gentleman—sensitive and aware of the broader scope of life but sadly lacking a sense of responsibility. After Mother and he divorced after 27 years of marriage, he seemed to be overwhelmed by life. Now, Carolyn's death seemed to take away what remained of his will to live.

When you lose a loved one, especially a parent or child, it is often not the conscious attachments to the deceased that takes time to process but the unconscious attachments. After dad died, I buried the pain for two years, yet I constantly felt him around me. I could feel the sadness and remorse he had over his life, which manifested as pain in my shoulder. Interestingly, when I finally let him go, the constant pain in my shoulder disappeared.

Healing my relationship with my father started when I realized he had disappointed me on many levels. On the Soul level, I knew we had been together in many different roles in many different lifetimes. In this lifetime, I was disappointed that I didn't get enough of his undivided attention. As a child, I was deeply lonely when his work took him away from home. And when he was home, I felt shut out. He always had his nose in a book, unraveling the mysteries of Atlantis, aliens, UFOs and the paranormal—a pre-disposure to psychic phenomena he received from his also gifted mother.

While grieving for my father, I sometimes felt an overwhelming desire to go home, to be with him again, to close the gap of separation. But our comings and goings from this earthly plane are part of this life's experience, even though there is comfort knowing that we are never apart on the Soul Plane. Knowing we will be rejoined with our loved ones someday in the Oneness of Spirit eases the Soul and allows true healing to take place.

Ten years after our father's death, Cecelia and I were talking on the phone. She said something, and then sighed. I felt the vibration of our father within her sigh, saying, "That sigh feels like Daddy is with us." Suddenly, he appeared to both of us as if we were all sitting in the same room. He put his arms around us and gave us a very specific message: "Find the joy in this life. In everything you do, find the joy. That is the real essence of your life."

It took ten years for my father to come to us, yet it happened quite naturally. Even though I deal with many beings on the other side, mostly for other people, dad had never appeared until then. I was overcome with joy, and I felt as though a long-closed tomb of sensitivity had finally opened to receive the gifts.

Three months after burying our father, Cecelia and I received another somber phone call. Our beloved stepfather, Bob, had just been diagnosed with cancer. He had been complaining for five years of aches and pain, but his doctors never took him seriously, nor did they ever check him for cancer. When the final diagnosis was made, he had only six weeks to live. Having just buried our father, it was a terrible blow.

Bob had married our mother fifteen years earlier. I had resisted him at first, but, over time, he was the one man who taught me the meaning of unconditional love. I had sought it from my birth father, and from men who claimed to love me. But even though I resisted Bob for many years, he was steadfast in his love for me and in his desire to be part of my life. I laugh when I think of him today—he gave me such grief about my "swami meetings" and which turban I chose to wear to the latest "séance." Bob never pretended to understand what Cecelia and I were up to with our meditation meetings and channeling seminars, but he was good-natured and accepting, and that was enough.

It was difficult to travel back and forth from Colorado to Mobile, visiting hospitals, funeral homes and grieving relatives—first for our step-mother, then our aunt, our father and step-father–all within a nine-month period.

Bob was in hospice care for nearly a month, all the while choosing not to face his terminal condition. When he asked Cecelia and me to visit him, we did, spending long nights sitting by his bed, seeing the fear in his eyes and witnessing his refusal to acknowledge his condition. Once an imposing man at 6' 7" tall, Bob was becoming a mere shadow of his former self.

It was when visiting his hospice room that a Guardian Angel appeared over our stepfather's head. It had a soft, feminine energy that felt unconditionally loving and immensely compassionate. Its soft, bright light glowed, sometimes transforming into rainbow colors. It seemed to be stroking Bob's energy field, unraveling his fears. The Guardian Angel instructed us to do the same.

Cecelia and I stood at Bob's head and feet, touching him lightly, allowing the angelic energy to pour through us into his body. Sometimes we were told to hold our hands over his abdomen to fill it with Divine Energy, comforting him while he dealt with painful memories. This process went off and on for days. We would go into connection, seeing the Guardian Angel's face and hands, allowing its energy to fill the entire room. It was our teacher, our friend and our mentor in learning how to work with Angelic Presence.

The Angel helped us guide our beloved stepfather to the other side, something neither of us could have done before. We prayed for help daily. Finally, the day came when Bob's eyes grew soft and calm. He never admitted his fate, but he was no longer afraid of it. For this, we were thankful.

Listening to Spirit has created many dramatic changes in my life. The move to Colorado put me in the right place at the right time for my future work. After working in the marketing and advertising departments at several radio stations, my guides told me to quit my job and write this book with Cecelia. In all-or-nothing style, I did it.

Several months after leaving the last station, I received an opportunity to host my own radio show. During seven years of learning the radio business inside and out, I had no idea that this might be part of my purpose, but it's good to remember that no matter where you are or what you do, there is always a higher plan at work.

Whether simply opening ourselves to our intuition or our psychic abilities, we are only given so much information about our lives. Perhaps knowing too many details in advance puts us in our own way. Spirit reveals its plan on a need-to-know basis, and, even then, it's only for those of us who are paying attention. Nevertheless, we are always being directed, if only we take the time to quiet ourselves and listen.

We are, indeed, like the aspen tree that becomes its most beautiful, golden self in the autumn—a time that feels as though life is waning. Instead, it is just a time when we are releasing everything we no longer need.

Chapter Six

GLASTONBURY ABBEY

I have a difficult time traveling because I tend to take on the energies of others, which can be mentally and physically exhausting. So when Cecelia and I visited the British Isles in 1999, we appointed Cecelia the designated driver and me the designated navigator.

While planning our trip, our Guides told us to forgo a specific itinerary, to make no reservations, to allow Spirit to lead us. That's how we were guided to stay at a 200-year-old farmhouse called Southridge Farm three miles from Glastonbury Abbey, the sight purportedly home to King Arthur, Queen Guenivere and mythical Avalon. Upon arriving, tired and frazzled from our journey, Cecelia and I chose to rent a room with a bath rather than a shower. Nothing sounded better than a hot soak to ease the tension of the day, which was caused by driving on the left side of the road and using left-hand auto controls. In addition, we needed to wash away the energetic imprints from many of the locations we had been visiting.

We arrived at Southridge Farm late on a Wednesday afternoon, unpacked the car and traveled down the road for dinner. We returned looking forward to the relaxation of our long-awaited bath. I was to bathe first, as Cecelia sat down to read and unwind from the day.

Feeling the warmth of the bath wash over me, I slid down in the tub to wet my hair, which fanned about my face in the water. After soaking for several minutes, I rose up to splash water onto my face when, suddenly, I had a frightening vision. I saw a severed head floating beside me in the water! The head appeared to have been torn from its body, ragged flesh around the neck. It had long brown hair and a mustache over full lips, and its eyes appeared to have been wide open at the moment of death. I was unnerved, rattled to my core. I was terrified to keep my eyes open but equally terrified to keep them closed.

When I found the courage to open my eyes, I was so relieved to find myself alone in the tub. Still, I kept my vision to myself so Cecelia could enjoy her bath in peace. But there was to be no peace. When she returned to our room after her bath, she had an odd look on her face.

"I just experienced the strangest thing," she said. "The whole time I was in the bath, I couldn't remember where I was, I couldn't remember my name and I couldn't remember anything about myself—even what my home looks like. I was really confused!"

It was then that I shared my experience with her. Afterward, we decided to energetically clear our suite, particularly the bath area. When we were finally sure we had been able to release this earth bound spirit we were able to enter into a peaceful—and long—sleep. Later Cecelia realized she was feeling the loss and isolation of the murdered spirit.

Glastonbury Abbey was an incredible homecoming for me. As I walked over the property where the grand altars once stood, it felt so familiar. I felt my body elongate, my spine open up to breathe. I had a sense of belonging, a sense of ownership. I began flashing on certain scenes, past vibrations of men of power and women subjugated in service. I felt the devotion of the cooks as they prepared the feasts of the day. I saw priests pointing pretty young girls into the priests' chambers, perceiving it was the duty of the maidservants to be available to the priests. (So much for celibacy!)

I saw a sign noting that the last Abbot of Glastonbury Abbey, before the troops of King Henry VIII began dismantling the country's abbeys, was a man named Richard. Just as I began to delve into the matter, I felt called to sit under some of the larger trees on the grounds. When I sat beneath them, I felt an odd familiarity, as if I had sat there many times before.

Cecelia and I stayed at Glastonbury Abbey for many hours, but every time we tried to go into a connection with Spirit, a tour group would come by, and it just didn't seem appropriate to channel in front of British school children.

Instead, we went into a nearby town for tea and cakes. We enjoyed them immensely, but we didn't enjoy the neon, pseudo-spirituality that characterized the streets of Glastonbury. It had a carnival feeling, underscored by a large number of street vendors, jugglers and clowns—a total contrast to the pure energy of the Abby.

Still, we carried on. Next, we visited the Tor, an ancient hill that is the site of mystical celebration and folklore. Because the walk to the site was long and steep, we stopped to rest and talk with other visitors on their way down, two of whom were a couple from Texas who made a pilgrimage there every year. Eventually struggling to the top, we looked out over the rolling hills and valleys from the high vantage point of the Tor and were struck by the view. It was instantly clear how the King Arthurian tales of Avalon, home to Camelot's high priestesses, and its islands, ghosts and misty veils had come about. When the moor was flooded, there was no way to get to the Tor but by boat.

In the ruins of St. Michael's Church, which rests at the top of the Tor, I discovered a plaque noting, to my amazement, that this had been the execution site of Richard, the last Abbot of Glastonbury. He had been savagely beheaded, his head stuck on a lance, his limbs torn from his body and his parts scattered over the area. I knew then that it was Richard's head I had seen in my vision at the inn.

PART II
CECELIA'S PATH

Chapter Seven

ON THE EDGE

Do not be afraid to reach out to your angels. Expect to be helped, and all manner of blessings will flow into your life.

—Cecelia Keenan

For as long as I can remember, I have been filled with a longing for some unnamed connection with a Being whose identity was just beyond my grasp. I can remember knowing there was more to living than what I was seeing. Even as a child, I felt some kind of connection to things I didn't have the consciousness to understand.

I had a personal experience with an Angelic Being after being hit by a car at age five. This Being was kind and loving like my grandmother. It was able to soothe my pain and release the fear I was feeling. I had been taught that if I ran into the street and a car hit me, I would die. I believed my life was over. Because of this, my special Angel would visit me at night to reassure me otherwise, often while my mother or father was sleeping in the same room. The Being, who had a feminine energy, communicated to me that I had agreed to come to earth in this lifetime to do many things. She told me she knew how difficult it was to be on the earth plane but that one day I would understand why. She also told me that if I would agree to stay and complete my mission, she would always be with me. Apparently I agreed to the Being's request because I am still here many years later.

I struggled during the year after the accident because my injuries required a great deal of healing and recovery time. I remember thinking I would never be out of pain. My jaw had been broken and wired back together, the skin on my back had been scraped nearly clean, my right leg had broken and I had a steel pin below my right knee. I endured a body cast and long months of physical therapy to gradually build up the strength to walk again. I am sure that at a purely physical level, I often regretted agreeing to remain and deal with all of this pain.

For many years after the accident, I suffered from medical complaints that often had to be resolved through surgery. It seemed all the joy of living had gone out of my young life, and I was angry. After the accident, I never returned to my dancing lessons, which I had loved. In addition, my sister Nancy and I started attending a private Christian school in Mobile, Alabama, that did not believe dancing was an appropriate activity for anyone. In fact, you were considered a sinner, with the threat of going to Hell for eternity, if you danced—or enjoyed almost anything else considered fun or normal in childhood.

Add to this the fact that I was convinced my parents were sinners because my father smoked and drank and because they attended Mardi Gras balls and other parties that promoted dancing. I spent a lot of my time fearing for their Souls and attempting to "save" them from themselves. I had been taught to see God as a hateful, vengeful being who would punish you if you did not do everything to His satisfaction. Worse, there was no discussion at home to balance the exceedingly negative teachings we were exposed to in school every day. Instead, we were taught that all people who happened to be born in the " wrong" country or into the "wrong" religion were doomed. No wonder I was sick and angry at the world, my parents and other people who did not understand the mortal danger they were in.

The result of these teachings was that I became quite aggressive early on as a way to gloss over my own fears, my feelings of not belonging and my sense of not being good enough to suit God. I don't believe my nervous system ever recovered from all the physical traumas caused by the childhood auto accident, and I forgot how to play and laugh. Even as a child, I became quite serious and didn't see much to feel happy about in the world around me. I had a few good friends during my youth, but I was basically an introvert and had a more difficult time making friends than my sister Nancy. As a result, I became quite addicted to reading—something I enjoy to this day—because, just for a while, I could escape into another world.

Reading exposed me to different experiences, viewpoints and belief systems. On some level, my young mind began to question everything around me. Eventually, I discovered a great attraction to the ancient Egyptians, the pyramids and early societies that had lived more closely in tune with nature or had strong connections to Spirit. Their deities were not always male nor were they necessarily punitive. I believe these insights provided me with enough raw material to open my mind, if not my heart, to new ways of thinking.

But I didn't receive much encouragement for pursuing my interests in ancient teachings, the possibility of alternate life forms and the paranormal except from my father. Instead, I hid these beliefs from my friends, held them close to my heart and tried to fit in with everyone else. I went through materialistic phases, looking for happiness. I pursued studies in college that would help me earn a living instead of awakening my passion for meaning in life. Eventually, all I wanted was a happy stable home life in a relationship with someone who loved me for myself. Instead I allowed myself to be what I thought others wanted me to be so they would love me. It took quite a long time for me to give myself permission to like myself and to recognize my own value.

It was not an easy task to stay in touch with feelings of worthiness. Early on, as the oldest child of five siblings, I understood that I was expected to be the one who would succeed. Perhaps this is not unusual for the first child; however, it can create a great deal of anxiety, particularly if in the depth of your Soul you don't feel competent. I remember thinking, "If I'm so smart, why can't I seem to get my life on track?" It would take many years to learn that it was on track, that it was all just a part of my journey.

In college, I earned a degree in Speech Pathology and began my first career in the public school system in Alabama. I was hired under a Federal Title I program, which meant I was not really part of any of the 21 schools I was expected to cover but an itinerant visitor. The over-crowded and under-financed school system rarely had a proper room in which I could work. I can remember trying to hold speech therapy sessions behind the curtains on a stage while other groups of children were eating lunch on the other side—you can imagine the noise level!

At another school, I held group sessions in a small open area outside the women's restroom, which witnessed continual traffic. It was difficult to concentrate on helping these children who so desperately needed attention. Many of them had speech or hearing impediments and seriously deficient language development. But, most of my work had to do with filling out government forms and doing mounds of paperwork rather than assisting the children. I was frustrated. Within five years, I was completely burned out. I didn't feel I was accomplishing anything or making any real difference in these children's lives.

A year later, my husband and I started our own interior design business, a completely new experience for me. For the first time, I had to go out and prospect for new business, both private and commercial. I had to learn to sell prospective new clients on our business, our products and on the two of us. This forced me to overcome any reluctance I once had of interacting with unfamiliar people or unfamiliar circumstances.

At the time we started our company, I thought I would only be working there for a short period of time. My husband told me I neither "had the personality" for sales nor did I have the experience. We had also just welcomed into the world our first child, daughter Lee, and I wanted to stay home with her.

However, within the first week of simply "helping" the business out, I made my first sale, and the rest is history: I was a success! But it should have been no surprise—I have always been able to do whatever I put my mind and energy into. In fact, anytime I am told I can't do something, you can be sure I'll do it.

Over the next 10 years, I became quite accomplished in the world of business, adding many new skills to my business toolbox. Despite this, I eventually sensed a void creeping back into my life. It seemed that no matter how much money I earned or how much I could buy or how often I got something I thought I really wanted, I felt a deep sense of dissatisfaction.

Instead of examining my dissatisfaction, I ignored these promptings from my Soul and continued to pretend that everything in my life was fine. All my energy went into suppressing my feelings, which made me tired. I had never allowed myself time off unless I was sick; it would never have occurred to me that I needed down time or had a need to listen to my inner voice. I had convinced myself that my husband and I needed our design business to support our family in the style to which we were accustomed. But I felt trapped. Yet whenever I tried to talk to my husband about the strain the business was putting on our relationship and on me, he either reacted with anger or became silent.

Instead of recognizing that my energy was being stolen a little bit every day, I allowed everyone else's feelings and fears to be more important than mine. Eventually, my husband and I decided to sell the business, and we found two couples who were interested. On the day we met with the potential buyers, I sat there and listened to my husband actually talk these people out of buying the business. It seemed that his fear of moving in a new direction prevented him from letting go of what was holding us both back. Naturally, I was upset. On the one hand, he said he wanted out of the business, but, on the other hand, he was shooting down our chance to walk away with money in our pockets and an opportunity for something else to come into our lives. He allowed his fear of the unknown be more powerful than his desire for us to succeed as couple.

After that, many negative situations came into our lives. Spirit had opened a door for us, but we didn't walk through it. Instead, we shut it. So it should have come as no surprise that the foundation of our business was rocked from within. Things began to happen, early warning signs of what was to come. Things disappeared from our warehouse with no visible signs of a break-in. Trusted employees were found to be underhanded in their dealings with our customers and us. Other employees lied to us about the scope of the jobs they were handling. Our best customers began having financial problems and could not pay us. Receivables were higher than ever, yet we couldn't collect them.

I had known at a very deep level that something wasn't right, but I couldn't get my husband to look more closely at what was happening. What good is it to have a gift if no one recognizes it, or, worse, they feel threatened by it? This was a frightening time for me, one of the darkest of my life. Everything my husband and I had worked so hard to build was either going or gone.

In the end, my husband and I lost nearly everything, and our children were bitterly disappointed in the lifestyle changes it required. While previous afternoons included lazy days at the country club enjoying couples tennis, current afternoons included struggle just to keep our lives together. In addition, there was the embarrassment and stigma associated with losing our livelihood and having to file bankruptcy. With such an experience, our sense of self worth and judgment was called into question, by us and by others. It was difficult to hold our heads up proudly. In fact, I will never forget going to court the day we had our bankruptcy hearing and recognizing the attorney for the state was a man I had known in high school. He had a difficult time looking at me, and I had a difficult time looking at him.

It was during this time we learned who our true friends were or weren't.

Eventually, my husband was offered a job by one of our former suppliers, which meant moving to Fort Collins, Colorado. In a way, it was a relief to be leaving our hometown so we wouldn't have to run into people we knew and feel their pity or scorn. Although much of this trepidation was in our own minds, we felt it intently.

We don't always know why bad things happen to good people, particularly at the time they happen. We wonder what we have done to deserve such a thing. We feel abandoned by those we trusted, hurt by the resulting loss of friends and the loss of an old way of life. We can't see that we will ever feel good about ourselves again. It is difficult to remember when something bad is happening that there are new people and new experiences waiting to come into our lives. It's the one-door-closing, other-door opening story: One door must close for another door to open.

It took a long time for me to understand this truth, but, in time, sunshine did melt away the storm clouds. Eventually, the reason for this hardship was made known to me, and I was able to see that the best can always be yet to come. But truth can take its own sweet time revealing itself, and I had to learn a great deal of patience along the way.

To date, I had been able to do almost anything I wanted to do. On the other hand, I was unable to maintain the high level of energy required to do so. I know now that this was a reflection of my ego needs and the needs of my Soul not being in alignment. I had always been willing to sacrifice the desires of my heart to live out someone else's vision for my life. The longer I subjected myself to this form of living, the weaker I became physically.

Once I removed myself from my hometown and my inappropriate situation, my energy began to return. I felt I had turned a corner for the better. I liked my new home in Colorado, and the children were settling in nicely. It seemed only a matter of weeks before I had met some new friends who had more in common with the real me than those people I had left behind. For the first time in years, I didn't have a job, and I began to explore my new world. On the weekends, my husband, my children and I would take the car to parts unknown and explore, just to see what we could find. The part of me that had been in hiding for most of my life was starting to re-emerge.

Imagine my disappointment when I realized that the more authentic I became, the more true to myself I was, the more distant my husband became. He told me he didn't like me anymore because I had changed, and he didn't understand why. The happier I became, the more depressed he became. We had only been in Fort Collins about six months when his father asked him to return to Alabama to help with his business. I couldn't believe he would even consider this, as he and his father had worked together before and it had ended badly. But he was convinced it was the right thing to do.

When he told me about his decision, I chose not to return to Alabama. My children did not want to leave, and I did not want to leave. My husband left and it became clear to me that our time together was over. We had been together for many years, but he still did not know the real me—and he didn't seem to want to. It was one of the most painful times of my life.

The path behind me seemed strewn with disasters—a failed marriage, a failed business and betrayals by friends I had loved and trusted. Added to that was the death of my father, stepmother, aunt and stepfather, all within a short time. There was a lot of emotional fallout, especially with my son, along with destroyed finances and problems resolving bankruptcy issues with the IRS. I was living in a new state, but my emotional support system was elsewhere. The stress and trauma of those years finally took their toll: I was diagnosed with Chronic Fatigue Syndrome, which I felt in every cell of my body. I was worn out body, mind and spirit.

I tried the traditional medical route to find a way to heal, but it soon became clear that this was not working. Few physicians believed I was truly ill; they felt my condition was psychosomatic. I had no doubt about the reality of my illness, but I grew tired of being questioned about the state of my mind. I was so beaten down by it that, as a last resort, I began listening to my inner knowing. I decided to take my healing into my own hands, exploring alternative methods to deal with my dis-ease.

It was through learning to heal my own body that the sleeping healer within me began to emerge. I exposed myself to many different healing modalities practiced by other cultures, exploring outside the traditional Western medical box, which opened my mind to many new possibilities.

After trying many different alternative healing modalities, I was introduced to Holographic Repatterning (HR). I felt more relief from just one HR session than I had received from any other modality. My interest was piqued, and I began to take classes with Chloe Wordsworth, the Creator of this incredible process. I then became a certified HR practitioner, working with many clients over a three-year period—a wonderful time for me, from which I learned many valuable lessons.

Learning Holographic Repatterning was the first of many steps that helped me reconnect with my intuitive self. The gifts hinted at during my early life were finally being recognized. I eventually allowed myself to be guided to many new methods of working with my clients. A whole new world was opening up to me. Best of all, I began to understand what my life—its lessons, its trials and its heartbreak—was about. I had just graduated from the 2x4 school of learning! I had gone through all these life trials in order to find a way to come out whole on the other side. It prepared me to be a more compassionate coach for those who were led to me. Once I fully committed to Spirit to use my gifts and to fulfill my purpose, Spirit assured me that I would never have to worry about where my clients would come from or how they would find me. Within two weeks of receiving this message, I was invited to a party in Denver where I met many people who would become important to me in my new life as an alternative healer and teacher.

Over the years I have created my own method of working with clients through partnership with the wonderful Healing Masters and Guides who assist me in all I do. I now realize that every curve ball life has thrown at me was to teach me compassion and to help me with my own growth. Adversity has taught me to "judge not." It has made me better at what I do and allowed me to find my own center. I know now that my illness was created over a long period of denial. I had blocked my own energy by ignoring the needs of my Spirit. I allowed the beliefs and feelings of others to become more important than the Inner Voice that was calling to me. My illness gave me the opportunity to look deeply inside myself, to open to my guidance and to reconnect with my life's purpose.

It has been my great joy to assist many wonderful people with their own healing process. But all healing is self-healing; I simply help others facilitate their own inner healer. By helping others, I have helped myself even more. I feel truly blessed by Creator and hope that this retelling of some of my journey will help those of you who feel you have lost your way. Know that you are never off your spiritual path, no matter how dark it may seem. Even those who do not know there is a path are nevertheless about the work of their Souls. No matter how far you feel you may have wandered from your course, there is always a way back to the light.

Do not be afraid to reach out to your Angels or trust your inner Knowing. Expect to be helped, and all manner of blessings will flow into your life.

Chapter Eight

INTER-DIMENSIONAL ARTISANS

I went to White Fish, Montana the summer after my first grandson, Bailey Starling, was born. He had a rough start, which caused us to use every healing power known to man or woman to keep him on this side. Nancy and I were present at his birth, which initially seemed to be fine. But by late that night, he had contracted a severe infection, and he was taken to a different hospital's pediatric intensive care unit, where he remained for several weeks. It was very touch and go for a while and there were people all over the country praying for his recovery. By the time he was out of the woods, I was worn out and looked forward to a rest. The Angels could now take care of Bailey while some friends and I went off for a little R&R. Sometimes the harshest circumstances lead us to the place we need to be in order to receive our next gift.

When my friends and I decided to take our R&R in Montana, I hoped to spend time connecting with nature in the mountains, but I didn't know if that would be possible. As it turned out, we did spend a great deal of time outside, allowing ourselves to be drawn to just the right place for sighting rare animals or seeing bear grass that only blooms once every seven years. It was glorious!

One day I heard a voice clearly say, "Cecelia, ask the others to go into town." My Guides wanted me to take time to meditate and perhaps channel some information. When I asked my friends for some time alone, they were very willing to oblige me, and I was left to myself for a few hours.

I felt compelled to go up the wooded hill that was directly behind our cabin. There, I found a rock outcropping where I could relax and meditate. It was a beautiful, sunshine-filled day with a gentle, sweet-smelling breeze. And as I felt myself being absorbed into my surroundings, I was left undisturbed, even by insects. My body relaxed, and I felt such calm inside. Although I didn't experience any overwhelming insights, I had a sense of belonging to my surroundings. After what seemed like only moments, I was back in full consciousness. But my watch indicated that almost an hour had passed.

I felt refreshed and whole as I returned to the cabin, but when I reached the back door, it was locked—even though I distinctly remember unlocking it before I left. When I walked around the cabin to the front deck, I found a beautiful hummingbird that had apparently just flown into the window. I didn't know if it was alive or not, but I knew I was supposed to run energy into its body through my hands to help revitalize it. However, after I ran the energy, the little bird was obviously very much dead. I sensed I was to leave the hummingbird where it was. I thought this odd, as we were in the woods, in the mountains, with all sorts of animals and insects roaming about. I was sure it would begin to decompose and attract them, but, again, I heard I was to leave it there. So I sat down on the deck to wait for my friends, who arrived within 30 minutes. I told them about my meditation, about being locked out of the cabin and about the hummingbird on the deck. They all walked over to see it, but were equally puzzled about why I was being told to leave it. But we did.

The next morning, as we were cooking breakfast, my eyes were drawn to a pair of circular shaped, gold filigree earrings my friend was wearing. I commented how much I liked them, with their round, flat, unadorned crystals in the center. We all agreed they were quite unique.

Immediately following breakfast, I felt the energetic tugging that often indicates my Guides want to communicate, so we gathered in the living room to hear their message. The gist of the message was that the hummingbird was there to teach me that things could be different than they seem. My guides encouraged me to study the hummingbird because it would teach me about myself.

When the message was complete, I happened to glance at the friend whose earrings I had just admired. Imagine how startled I was to see that the crystal in each of her earrings, plain only moments before, now carried the image of a perfectly shaped hummingbird! She was equally amazed, as she had owned the earrings for several years and the crystals had never had any sort of design on them.

Later, we walked to the deck to see if the little bird was still there, and it was—in all its perfection. Nothing had disturbed it. I was told once again to leave it there, so we did. In the afternoon, we went into town and met a wonderful couple that ran a retail shop with an angel theme. There, I came across a book that described the spiritual meaning of certain birds and animals, so I looked up the hummingbird. Among the most significant meanings is its representation of joy, healing, playfulness, independence and the nectar of life. The hummingbird is the most skillful flyer of all birds, able to fly forward, backward and sideways. I was also told that this little traveler is fearless and can actually move between dimensions and that it also symbolizes accomplishing the impossible, which is significant to me because so often I try to accomplish the impossible.

For days after, we left our little guest alone, and for days it remained there as if it had a protective dome over its body. It was never disturbed, and it never lost its fresh appearance. Finally, on the fifth or sixth day of our vacation, we were told to carry the hummingbird up to the rock outcropping where I had meditated. We offered a prayer of thanks to the hummingbird for sacrificing its life to give us visible proof that there are unseen forces at work all around us that cannot be explained in traditional terms. To honor the occasion, my friend gifted me with the earrings, which I wear to this day.

I am always amazed at the miracle of their creation and know that Spirit was speaking to me clearly at that time. If we but listen, we will often hear the voice of Spirit and see it manifest in our daily lives.

Chapter Nine

SPIRITUAL MAGIC

It is absolutely incredible how Spirit can work in our lives if we allow it the opportunity. We are often prompted to go to places or do things that seem strange at the time but can be life-changing if we allow ourselves the freedom to go with the flow of guidance. It has long been my intention to stay open to the prompting of Spirit. This has allowed many opportunities for growth I would otherwise have missed if I had not let my right brain lead me even further into the realm of spiritual magic.

The next event was one of those magical opportunities. In the late summer of 1998, United Airlines launched a non-stop flight from Denver to London. As part of their promotional campaign, they announced they would offer a certain number of round-trip tickets for $199 each, first come, first served. I knew the tickets would disappear quickly, so I never even tried to get one. But I could not get England out of my mind. I mentioned the promotion to Nancy, and I told her I didn't know why I was feeling so compelled to go, but the idea had dug in and wouldn't let go. Approximately two weeks later, two other airlines matched United Airlines' fare, but I was told these tickets were probably gone as well.

With my Guides urging me on, I asked Nancy if she would go to England with me. She agreed to go if I could manifest the tickets for $199. We put our heads together to decide on a time frame, and she felt October would work best for her. My guidance was a little more specific, telling me we needed to be there the second week of October. Armed with this information, I called airlines No. 1 and No. 2. They both informed me that all promotional tickets had been reserved within a few hours of their availability. A little less hopeful about our prospects, I called airline No. 3 and asked if they had any promotional tickets to England left. A very kind lady said they were gone, but they had another deal about to be announced for $398 round-trip tickets to England. Even though I realized it was a bargain, I'm sure I sounded disappointed. I told her we wanted to go but only if we were able to buy the tickets for $199. For some reason, this stranger must have been guided to help us because, although she admitted she wasn't supposed to, she did. She put her computer on search, and it came up with two seats at the $199 price. They were leaving the second week of October and returning ten days later. Needless to say, we snapped them right up. Obviously, our Guides wanted us to go to England for a reason.

Our Guides later told us that we would be visiting sacred sites around the countryside but not necessarily those marked on a tourist map. We were asked to keep our itinerary loose, as we would be guided along the way. Our Guides said our destination was not London but the English countryside, where we would be reunited with some old friends along the way. Everybody thought we were foolish to go without arranged accommodations, but we felt quite confident that everything would work out just as it needed to.

From the very first day of the trip we encountered helpful, friendly people who would in some small way contribute a piece of information or advice that would lead us to the next important location on our journey. It seemed as though we were uncovering little pieces of ourselves as we traveled. An ancient memory here, a flash of insight there, a sprinkling of connection to our surroundings—all contributed snippets of awareness about us. Ultimately, we were to discover that the sacred sites we were visiting were parts of ourselves. Pieces of who we are and who we were came flooding into our awareness, altering our vision of ourselves, shining a new light of understanding within us and clarifying many of our present-day relationships.

The history of my family in this lifetime is tied to many different countries. Not all of our ancestors are from the same, or even similar, background. As far as I know, we can trace our roots to England, Ireland, Scotland, France and Native America. This is not unique to our family, so why is it important? Why do we feel a pull to one place over another or have a sense of comfort when visiting a foreign land?

Many of the immigrants who came to America were looking for a more prosperous way of life. Some were escaping religious or legal persecution. Others were shipped off against their will with little or no choice about their emigration to a new country. Upon arrival, they usually found themselves at the bottom of the economic barrel. They dressed differently, spoke differently and knew little of the culture they were about to adopt. They encountered the same suspicion and prejudice often directed toward those different from the status quo. It was difficult for them to gain acceptance in their new land. They endured grief, pain, suffering and loneliness—emotions we carry in our cellular memories because they are part of our bloodline.

Many of us have felt at one time or another that we didn't fit in, we didn't belong, we were misunderstood or alienated—just as immigrants to America must have felt. Imagine the feeling of moving to a new land, separating from family and loved ones, knowing you would likely never see them again. There were no cell phones, airplanes or Internet providers to keep them in touch with their former life. They must have felt great fear about survival, and, to cope, they shut down their hearts so they wouldn't feel how they really felt. They energetically felt disconnected from life—and from themselves.

The conditions that create our ancient cellular memories may no longer exist, but we are left to deal with the unresolved conflicts from which they originated. Many of the thoughts, feelings and beliefs from those memories are part of our subconscious programming. It may take generations to heal the constricted energy from our genetic history.

Every area on this planet has its own signature vibration that defines its uniqueness. This energy can be seen, felt and experienced at a deep cellular level. That is why we may feel energized in a particular place or country, especially one where we have hereditary ties, literal or cellular, direct bloodline or soul level connection. It may make us feel like we are reconnecting to a sleeping part of ourselves, awakening our senses, being emotionally pulled to certain areas of the planet. This churning of energy can trigger long-suppressed memories or awaken us to a missing piece of ourselves. It can create a heightened sense of awareness or it can be the catalyst for a new channel of inspiration.

Our physical bodies may still be trying to adapt to the energies of a region that is different from those in our ancient past. If our genetic makeup was adapted over a long period of time in a cold, wet climate, it may take several generations before we acclimate to a dry, desert location. We are a bio-energetic life form that is forever adapting and changing.

If our family history has been tied to poverty and backbreaking labor, we may still be dealing with a subconscious belief that we are not entitled to another kind of life. The history of earth as we know it overflows with examples of one group being enslaved by another or being forced to provide for others' needs at their own expense. This has contributed to the innate belief that the world is not a safe place, which is at the core of many of our fears around scarcity and lack of abundance.

Many of our ancestors' religious beliefs and attitudes have also contributed to our deeply held fears. On a deep level, we are still afraid that the God of our religion will punish us if we wander outside the belief system of our family or culture. This rigidity limits us and disallows a free and open communion with our own powerful connection to Spirit. Freeing ourselves from our past allows us to develop a new relationship with the place we live. So many of us have lost our connection to the earth and our desire to be here. It often requires exposure to new energy to give us a different perspective and help remove the blocks that prevent us from moving forward. Revisiting our past can often help us choose new directions that are more supportive of what we want and need now.

Our journey to England was just such an energetic catalyst for Nancy and me. It made us aware of many past lifetimes and their impact on our lives today. It helped us fill in gaps in understanding our present feelings and beliefs. It also gave us an opportunity to spend time with one another, sharing our past and consciously deciding how it should or should not impact our futures. We are both grateful for this experience and the expanded perspective it provided.

Each of us needs to pay attention to the places that call to us. There is most likely a reason we are being guided to a particular destination. Our experiences there may provide new energy to help open a dormant part of ourselves that is ready to be recognized and understood. Perhaps there will be someone we need to meet or something special we need to see. No matter the reason, we will be enriched by the experience and feel a new connection to our expanding role as planetary citizens. We are connected to all people, places and creatures—to all things.

Chapter Ten

VISIONS OF THE GARDEN

While visiting the garden isle of Kauai, Hawaii in 1997, I began to experience visions of the past. Each morning, I meditated on a high bluff overlooking the beautiful Pacific Ocean. As the sun began to rise, I could feel the energy of the island awaken a feeling in me of a very deep connection. There was a part of my ancient past vibrating itself into consciousness. I began to see the island as it must have appeared long ago. I saw myself walking under giant tree roots whose impressive height compared to that of today's elephants. The leaves and stems of native plants contained every color imaginable. Flowers over five feet in diameter graced the branches of surrounding flora.

As I saw myself walking through this garden-like space, I knew that the landmass on planet earth was once one gigantic continent of indescribable beauty and grandeur. The air was completely untainted by air or noise pollution. A delicate perfume permeated the environment, which subtly altered itself as I entered each new area. The verdant life around me nurtured my body, and I knew I needed nothing else to keep my form in a state of perfect balance and harmony.

Communion with all life forms was telepathic, and there was no fear among the various species residing there. All needs were met in a way that created a sense of satisfaction and completeness within the physical form. The rivers and lakes were free and natural, and the oceans were filled with intelligent life. The whales taught me of all that had been, and the dolphins taught me of all that was to come.

I found myself easily interacting with these original planetary citizens in a profoundly deep and respectful way. Telepathically they communicated to me that we humans were only now, in the past few decades, reawakening to our interconnection with all life forms. For millennia, human amnesia has kept us from knowing our True Selves, which has unbalanced the energy of the planet. As earth began to feel the influence of humanity, now gathered into individual tribes, her balance was affected. These concentrations of human energy began to negatively affect the interaction of other life forms. What was once a harmonious planet was becoming unbalanced by too much negative human energy. This gradually set the stage for the breaking up of the landmass. Over time, what was once whole became fragmented. I felt the pain of this separation in the deepest recesses of my psyche; it was like being cast out of the Garden of Eden. I felt that this was the beginning of our sense of separation from Creator, the loss of our spiritual unity. When we lost our deep connection to earth and all living things, we began to struggle for survival. What once we held title to, all that was highest and best, we lost through our own actions as a species.

On this same trip to Kauai, I communicated yet again with the whales as I had in the distant, distant past. My then-future husband, Tom Keenan, and my brother, Jim, and I decided to take a whale-watching tour one afternoon. The day was beautiful, but the ocean swells around the island were quite large. Our boat was stable, but we spent most of the day rough-riding waves. This made it difficult to see very far, and our hopes of sighting whales were slim. One woman on the boat told us, with tears in her eyes, that she and her husband were returning to New Zealand the following day, and they were so disappointed not to have seen a whale.

At that moment, I felt I should try to telepathically call the whales, something I had never done before. I told Tom about my feeling, then closed my eyes and pictured a whale until I sensed I had made a connection. Then I telepathically communicated to the whales, mind to mind, that we would feel honored to be in their energy field and asked if they would come near enough for us to see them. Then I opened my eyes, hoping that I had not appeared foolish to my husband-to-be as I desperately tried to contact whales!

Imagine my joy when minutes later someone spotted the spray from the blowhole of a whale not far from the side of the boat. Suddenly a beautiful, gray whale breached near our boat for several minutes. The woman from New Zealand cried tears of joy, and I felt a deep sense of validation about following my feelings. It was only later that I allowed my rational mind to question whether this was "just a fluke," no pun intended.

The next day, I decided to see if I could recreate this experience while sitting in my meditation spot on the ocean bluff. I was delighted to find I was again able to make a psychic connection with a whale, and I asked if it would help me validate my experience. Once again, I was gifted with the presence of a beautiful being from the sea. I sensed it was a male, and he stayed around for a long while before moving on. I repeated this process one final time before we left Kauai to offer my gratitude for the gift and to affirm that an old part of myself had reawakened to the connection we have to all living things.

Many of us have stories about reconnecting to Spirit that we need to share with others so we can enjoy the beauty of feeling connected to all living things.

PART III
THE TEACHINGS

INTRODUCTION
TO THE TEACHINGS

*You are as unlimited as time and space and are vast
reservoirs of collective awareness and experience.*
—Our Guides

With these profound words, our guides introduced the concepts that would be the foundation for the discourses presented here. By addressing the evolution of humanity in reference to family and relationships, by seeing who we are and where we come from, we begin to grasp the power we have to create our spiritual destiny. We are powerful beyond measure. We have only to awaken to the reality of our sovereignty to claim the consciousness of divinity that is our birthright.

By growing in compassion, consciousness and spiritual maturity, we find that we already have everything we need to complete our earth missions. Everything we need is right inside each and every one of us. We are our own unlimited resource. There is no limitation to what can be accessed, created and brought forth in the form of information or physical manifestation. We have found that traveling freely between dimensions is more than just a possibility; it is a reality. We have help from more sources than we can comprehend. Our universe is a loving home welcoming us as full participants in the evolution and transformation of All There Is.

As the 1990s drew to a close, Nancy had received specific inner direction to quit her job and devote her time everyday to receiving information for this book—not an easy task to surrender to. We were to be given information containing Universal Wisdom that would be of great benefit to many people.

We agreed to be channels for this information, even though we had no clear understanding of what the nature of the material would be. What we did know was that we had absolute faith in the intent and purpose of the messages. Over the last ten years, we have been given multiple opportunities to experience love and the acceptance that flows to us from our non-physical teachers and guides. The messages have been nonjudgmental, objective and nurturing—Spirit's way of allowing us to feel fully connected to Creator and Universal Creativity.

Any information that brings any of us down or causes us to feel fearful or doubt our inherent value and the value of love comes from ego, not Spirit. We have been led to understand that Wisdom never creates confusion. Universal Truth rings a bell of clarity that creates peace and optimism for the future. Notice whether you feel a sense of comfort from reading these messages or if you are prompted to take a different path. The choice is always yours.

The Guides, Angels and Ascended Masters responsible for these beautiful teachings asked that we record the words given to us as closely as possible to the way they were received. Although we have edited these messages somewhat for clarity, the basic messages are the same.

Messages in each chapter are often a combination of several guided sessions, but there is positive intent in the way the words work together, and transformative frequencies are encoded in the messages. It is not intended that the entire relevance of the content be understood as they are being read. In fact, it seems there is a time-delay component to these messages. As we continue to raise our personal vibrations, these codes will be triggered within the natural intelligence of our physical systems. These messages are simply intended to be a catalyst for our ascension into Higher Consciousness, with an understanding of what is available to us through the process.

Acceptance of the perfection in Universal Timing becomes clear as you reflect on your journey. You realize you have never been a victim and that you have been responsible for all the experiences you have drawn into your life. They may not have been pleasant ones, but they are those necessary for your Soul's evolution. It allows you to see the portions of yourself yet to be healed, particularly from experiences that repeat themselves until you get that great illuminating, "Ah-ha!"

If you are drawn to these messages and feel them being activated, you may benefit from reading this material more than once. You will know when it is time to once again pick the book up. This is not required in order for you to receive the full benefit of the material, but it will enhance the speed at which the coding will be completely activated within you. Coding refers to specific frequencies that activate the shifting cellular vibration of your genetic history. It enables you to know, on a deep level, Truth as it is presented. It empowers you to know who you are and to be able to act on that knowledge, becoming aware of what is being guided through your physical being.

The coding is intended to provide spiritual nourishment for your physical body as it undergoes its transmutation and to release discordant energies deeply embedded in the collective consciousness of humanity. This is a glorious service for each of you to provide for your fellow man, for the healing of the Self is the pathway to healing the planet. It can only begin from within. Personal and planetary ascension is your destiny, as you are all Spiritual Beings inhabiting physical bodies. Ascension occurs when you have allowed Spirit to fully move through you, to surround you, to guide your thoughts and actions. It occurs when you accept and surrender to your Soul experience as teacher, guide, lover and companion. Those of you focusing on raising your consciousness are catalysts for raising the consciousness of humankind. You are each needed to fulfill the promise of your Souls' evolution and to make a positive difference in the outcome of the destiny of all humanity, and thus the universe.

You are now at the proverbial crossroads. You are in a position of such power and vulnerability that each choice you make for love, for wellness and integrity are literally affecting the outcome in this historical era of human evolution. Join us with a loving, compassionate heart of Unconditional Love. Hold the positive belief that your only possible outcome is one of light. Speak Truth and the knowledge of your Soul in a forthright manner. Participate!

Our helpers in the unseen realms wish to acknowledge each of you Earth Angels, Light Workers, seekers and finders who curiously push forward for the benefit of all. They appreciate you for opening to the possibility of unseen realities so that you may perceive yourself as part of a much greater whole than previously imagined. They are aware of the difficulty and courage required to be forerunners and want you to know they send you Unconditional Love. They ask that you strive to keep your hearts open to receive the love and peace that is always available to you. Accept your treasure of unlimited resources from the Divine, and reclaim your natural inheritance from The One.

Chapter Eleven

THE ANCIENT ONES

Early in 1997, Cecelia and I sat down to receive our channeled message for the day and began discussing what these Guides might be. What were they, and why did they wish to come in through us? It is one thing for us to be willing to be channels, but what was *their* intention, *their* desire?

Before we connected with the Ancient Ones, we spoke the following prayer: "May all information we receive come from the highest levels of healing, love and light. Neither entities of darkness nor manipulation may enter these proceedings."

The Channeling Begins

Nancy: *We are a spiritually oriented race of beings that have visited and worked with the human inhabitants of this world for millennia. We are responsible for many of the scientific discoveries that have been attributed to the mind of man. We are the inspiration for many of the writings and drawings you have seen on the walls of the Ancient Pyramids and the symbols created on the tablets of the ancient societies. We are also the architects of the pyramids. We are the Fathers of Time who have worked with members of the White Brotherhood, among others, to bring forth our messages to those who are ready and willing to hear. We are asking for help and cooperation with* *our efforts, for we do wish to work through those who can be an intermediary between your world and ours. We appreciate your willingness to hear our message and your assistance in recording our words so they may be of benefit to the unfolding Universal Plan.*

Cecelia: *There has been a great deal of personal sacrifice by those who have been willing to heed our guidance. Many of your species who have seen our planetary representatives have been perceived as suffering from delusions or mental disorders. Many have been labeled charlatans for their efforts. That which cannot be proven by science has always been a great source of fear among those who need to be guided by others. Many who have given away their personal power have done so in the name of religious dogma related to control of one group by another.*

There have been many attempts to soften the consciousness of the human mind over the years. Many times, we have made great strides in creating a willingness to open to a more positive awareness in the minds of man, only to see a counter-productive campaign created by those who wish to see things remain the same. Quite often, movies or books will be released that engender a fear of aliens as devils who would take over the planet to dominate and enslave the human population. Many works of fiction have been created to counterbalance the positive intent of our messages.

It is time for humans to consciously acknowledge that you are not alone in your world. There are many other beings that are your brothers. There are those who are not interested in acquiring your worldly goods, altering your genetic structure or enslaving and utilizing you against your will. This is not, nor has it ever been, our goal or purpose.

In love and joy, we come to you to speak the messages for our group and to tell you of what is to come. We are in a process of up-leveling your energetic wiring in order for you to receive messages that carry a higher frequency and color. There are many frequencies that have been unavailable to you due to the limitations of your physical body. The frequency bands you can receive are tied into what your inner and outer senses can perceive. As you are being transmuted to higher levels of awareness, so, too, are your abilities to receive increased energy so your reception cannot be altered or tampered with. You see, depending upon the frequency level of the information you are receiving, there is currently a possibility that these messages may be bent or slightly altered by beings that can perceive these transmission bands. However, once you have been re-calibrated to a certain energetic level, others will no longer be able to see or bend these messages away from their intended form. You and each one of the light Workers who are here to anchor these new energies on the planet are unique unto yourselves. You carry a signature vibration that links you specifically with those who are also working in union with your mission. It often requires many years to find your unique signal, as it tends to become muted or covered over by the many denser vibrations that are all around you in every moment. This is why it is much easier for us to help you refine your own being on your own schedule, when you set aside specific time for us to work with you. Otherwise, we often have no option but to send our transmissions during your rest time when there is less outside interference. There is always "mind chatter" around you when you are up and about your everyday lives. This is why we encourage you to become diligent and devoted to the time you set aside for our interactions with you.

We are in the process of downloading new information for you to bring through and are also assisting you in cleaning out your old files (memories and feelings) that no longer serve you or your present level of understanding. You are being upgraded and revised so that your reception is much faster and the time that it takes to process new information is greatly reduced. This will become more important in the weeks and months ahead.

All Beings of light are in a gathering mode, and we are assisting all of our earthly counterparts in integrating new information more quickly so it can be utilized as soon as it is needed. Time is speeding up, as are the events on the planet. It may seem as though you have no sooner moved through one major event only to have another one take its place. That's because time is no longer stretching out in a linear fashion but is drawing back in on itself as it begins its return journey back to Source.

Time has been stretched out as far as it can go in this cycle, and it is now necessary to collect all the data from this dimension and all alternate dimensions as well. When complete, all experiences in physicality will be pulled back into the Collective Memory. This enables great decisions to be made by those Evolved Beings whose role it is to be the Masters of Time. They determine the next great cycle of experience and reassign those who have evolved to a higher level of consciousness to their next great mission for All There Is.

You are all here to learn to experience and reflect Divine love as it expresses through us. As you evolve, you become more filled with this powerful energy. It holds together your creations and allows you to become love in action. Divine love is not to be mistaken for romantic love, though all love contains Divine Love. But being filled with Divinity feels like falling in love. Divine love is the spark of the Creator that is contained within each one of you. It allows you the freedom to experience physicality as you evolve into conscious Beings of light.

Creator has great confidence in you and knows that all of your experience will contribute to the ultimate good of All There Is. Through your willingness to share your love and light, you allow humanity and your celestial family an opportunity to work together as co-creators for the benefit of all. When humanity is ready, many of you will serve as ambassadors between the species. This will be a time of great joy for the people of earth as they join forces with the higher realms. We look forward to that time with great anticipation and desire. We are anxious to be reunited with our children who have been journeying for eons. We are ready to welcome you all Home and help you ease through your transition into your celestial family.

You are all sons and daughters of the Infinite One. You carry the spark and energy of the Divine love that powers the universe within you. You are here for Self-ordained purpose and to help establish all that is for positive good into the vibrations of this physical plane.

Our words and our acts of kindness will draw those of you who recognize our messages. You cannot yet know what is planned for you, but you can carry a sense of peace within, knowing that you will be guided each step of the way. Your own spiritual blueprint is being followed and unfolded in accordance with Universal Timing and the parameters of your own life-goal project.

We would like, at this time, to speak through Nancy. We would like you to ask her if she would be willing to allow us to speak through her. Nancy can feel our vibrations and judge for herself whether or not she feels we are worthy of her interest and her help.

Nancy: *Go ahead. I am ready.*

Cecelia: *Please identify yourself.*

Nancy: *We are the Allron energies.*

Cecelia: *And you are the ones who created the pyramids and many of the historical aspects of this particular planet?*

Nancy: *We are not the only ones, however we are depicted quite often within these frameworks.*

Cecelia: *What about the movie "Contact?" Was it accurate?*

Nancy: *The duality of machinery in the movie, the public machinery versus the one used later, is an example of how your government creates one spaceship, one Mars landing, for the public view and another real one from which they are extracting actual information. This has happened over and over again. The original Moon landing was a staged presentation shown to the world. The real mission to the Moon included gathering information and exploring the entity in a way the government was unwilling to make known at that place and time.*

Cecelia: How do you explain the psychic images that some people claim to see that are not seen by others?

Nancy: The appearance of insanity in an individual is frequently, no more than their energy residing in a slightly different dimension. From the perception of that being, reality is what exists in that different dimension. However, those who view this behavior are in judgment of that particular level of awareness and are the ones who see them as insane.

The behavior of the clinically insane versus those who see alternate realities is very different. Those who are truly insane cannot control what information is coming to them, and they do not have the ability to filter inappropriate messages. They have wide-open channels with no controls and no filtering system. Understanding the inter-dimensional aspect of perception is very important because they are opening to higher levels of energy reception.

Cecelia: Let's talk more about the movie "Contact."

Nancy: The depiction of energetic tunnels is very close to the way actual travel through the wormholes is accomplished. It is quite accurate in terms of how the sensation of flying and being pulled through feels. Many movies and TV shows are being created that depict inter-dimensional travel in an accurate way. We are guiding the Creators of these movies, books and presentations to provide you with an accurate sensory experience. Many of these writers think they have a very active imagination, but they are simply plugging into a powerful resource and presenting Truth that is, in fact, stranger than fiction. Who could create such a thing as the reality you have all experienced thus far? You are only just beginning your travels. Your expectations of what will come will not be limited by your imaginings but will be fueled by the fire within your Soul and your eagerness to learn what is to come.

We cannot pour all of our knowledge into one individual or one brain at the same time. Instead we are giving bits and pieces of the puzzle to various individuals so the information can be merged and blended at the appropriate time. In one assembled group, we might use one or two primary speakers to give different information to each person; other members of the group will be given thought suggestions, vibration resonance and frequency shifts to accompany those doing the speaking. It all works together in a mosaic, a pattern that is spinning at all times to create the Truth that is unfolding before your eyes

All manner of creative expression will be enhanced by the new frequencies. As you channel in higher spiritual frequencies, you may find yourself accessing unknown musical ability or a talent for sculpting, writing or any of the arts. All energy will be given in such a way that you may access the highest expressions of those art forms.

We are the Ancient Ones. We are the Elders who, at the beginning of each new era, come forth to instruct you and show you the way. Early on, our earthly representatives may be seen as the rebellious ones, carrying messages of discontent, screaming out for change and attempting to forge a new future from the past, always on the leading edge. But we are at the front lines, giving direction and inspiration to humanity in its deepest hour of discontent. We always return to offer our help. We resurface during the middle of an Age and then again toward the end of an Age as it begins to fade. Before we leave, we help humanity emerge into yet another new phase of living in its evolutionary process.

We carry the stars on scepters and arrange planetary positioning. We create such energies as your sun shining forth to lead you out of darkness and into new day's light. We provide the seeds within the earth and the running waters. We give back all energies of life and nurturing as the Mother Earth. We combine these energies as the Father and come forth as Spirit Guides and as human leaders.

It is from Starship IV that we circle and watch over the energies of this planetary system and send down information. We project a physical image to those who are willing to grasp our messages and allow them to be presented. We can send vibrational intelligence through thought forms or we can wake you in the middle of the night with a feeling. We might tap you on the shoulder in any place, quite literally, to get your attention. It is not important that we actually stand before you or that we actually speak words in your language from voices that appear similar to your own. We are always aware, in total clarity, of the condition of your planet and are able to send whatever information is needed at any time. We do hesitate, however, to interfere in the action phase of your planetary "karma." (This is not a word we particularly like but understand that it is resonant with your understanding of the issue. As you create an action, you create a reaction in response to it.) We attempt to stay out of karmic energy flow, but we let you know that we are available for assistance at any time you ask.

We have created miracles within this world that have been attributed to the Christed One and to others, for truly we have worked through many humans or human embodiments on this planet. Many miracles have been credited to certain ones of the earthly plane, but there are also many unknown individuals we have worked through. In the miraculous healings and "parting of waters," or in the stopping of such natural disasters as earthquakes and fires, we have performed miracles through any number of common humans throughout history. For those who have been the beneficiary of the miracles, we say, "Rejoice." Now you know or may begin to see that the grander activities of Spirit combined with your energy are indeed present in your everyday life.

We ask you to turn your attention upward and connect to the intensity of the energies we are sending. We are offering more expanded interactions to help with the confusion that is in your world today. When you are being tapped on the shoulder, it may be one of your personal Guides or it may be us. We will always be there for you. Know that many of you are here to perform many feats of seeming improbability through your understanding and willingness to assist in the evolution of your own species. We do applaud and congratulate all efforts and will be ever in assistance on this matter.

Cecelia: *Are you the energies that are sending us the information that we are recording for the book?*

Nancy: *Yes, in part. There are many groups assembling at different points to send the information that is required. You see, you have to live the experience and to open certain passageways for the higher information and understandings to come through. But were these not connected to the physical reality you are living daily, it would have little impact on any other person walking in your own time frame.*

Cecelia: *Can you tell me the reason for the original connection with us after the first viewing of the movie "Contact?"*

Nancy: *As was just stated, you must have earthly references to information you are receiving at all times to validate and confirm them. It was a prime opening, was it not, to speak to you on subject matter that was most predominant in your minds at that time?*

Cecelia: *Absolutely.*

Nancy: *You have needed much reassurance.*

Cecelia: *That's true. Am I getting beyond that?*

Nancy: *There are days.*

Cecelia: *You have stated, twice now, that we will, within the next two years, have a face-to-face encounter. Is this an actual event or is this something else?*

Nancy: *You have had face-to-face encounters already. You will continue to have face-to-face encounters with entities unlike yourself. You do not recognize the entities by the faces they wear, only by the energy they carry. If we will turn to the screen version for one moment, you did see how it was enacted. It was not entirely accurate regarding (when you saw the) father, yet it was quite similar in the ways these energies were presented to you in human form with recognizable faces. They come in to speak only a word or two or to emit an energetic frequency in your presence. It may come through as a taste on the back of the tongue or a resonance within your own lung system or* *within your heart, your hearing range—certainly within your sense of smell or touch. You are receiving information in many ways; understand that it is all with purpose.*

Cecelia: *So the formaldehyde smell I have encountered several times is an example of this?*

Nancy: *Yes.*

Cecelia: *So the smell was not actually a chemical release?*

Nancy: *Life is a living, breathing, existence that is never dull or static. It is always shifting and changing, bringing in and magnetizing, sending off and repelling in such vast transition that when anything stabilizes even for one second, it is really quite surprising. You cannot imagine the incredibly strong belief system that does hold things in place for you long enough to feel satisfied with what you will call your now-time experience.*

Cecelia: *Are you the Ancient Ones that I perceive as having white robes, beards and hair?*

Nancy: *Sometimes we are green or other colors.*

Cecelia: *Yes, but I usually see you as white. Are you the same group I saw standing on stage with our arms held high in salute?*

Nancy: *Indeed.*

Cecelia: *That's what I thought. You are our Fathers, are you not?*

Nancy: *Indeed.*

Cecelia: *We are your children?*

Nancy: *Welcome Home! You are we, and we are you. We are family.*

Cecelia: *I feel it now, the emotion is coming up, the recognition, and I just didn't have a name for it before. You are the Elohim?*

Nancy: *That is one name. You humans are very tied to naming and labeling energies of light. The issue of labeling who the messenger is tends to break the thought form, the flow of energy. The labeling is like trying to name the wind that is blowing through the room. As soon as you are in a place long enough to name it, it has already gone.*

Chapter Twelve

BEYOND THE
ILLUSION

We are all works of art in progress, with transitions influenced by the changing hand of Creator. When one of us shifts our perception to raise our vibration, we have influenced the whole of Creation.

In one of the earliest channeling sessions, the following transmission was received through Nancy, as Cecelia took notes. A tape recorder was also used, for the material flowed faster than Cecelia's note-taking skills would allow.

Nancy: In the beginning, there was unformed, shapeless, pure essence. As the world started coming together, there was the necessity for form to be sealed with structure and relativity—one thing, place and person to another thing, place and person. For eons before human beings walked planet earth, there were life forms in all areas, shape-shifting and forming into different species and civilizations. You will understand, through this discourse, that all human experience has been about coming together for examination of contrasts and for learning.

Whether expressing good or evil, dark or light, the contrast has been the manner through which you humans limited your experience yet stopped to look at both sides of the coin. You formed your concepts of right or wrong by how each experience felt to you. You began to associate your actions and the actions of others with the pain or happiness you felt. Emotions were felt within the physical form as a result of your activities. Humanity was being programmed by its own actions. The Soul within the physical form became less and less Self-aware.

This was all part of the Divine Plan. It was known that one day, when humankind had experienced all that was needed for personal learning, the God-Spark within each of you would re-ignite. Mankind would begin the transmutation back into the Unlimited Resource that it is.

We are here to help reawaken those of you who are ready for the Truth of yourselves. As you begin to feel the power of the vibration of Universal Energy that exists within you, you feel the expansion of Self and realize the unlimited nature of your own being. You are capable of touching, affecting and completing all things energetically. In the past, you have limited yourselves, but the time has come for realization to be with you. There are many more things of an expanded Universal Nature for you to do now. All sense of what you have been able to accomplish in the past is being erased from your memory bank and is being replaced with a higher knowledge and expanded information about the Unlimited Resource that you are. This Unlimited Resource is there for all.

In the beginning, you made a commitment to this reality. Your contract was to become an Unlimited Resource. This shift in vibration requires being at the right place and time in your development to allow yourself to open these channels. Once open, you may become an anchoring point of in-flowing and out-going energy. This requires a tremendous leap of faith in the physical-plane reality where you exist. We are telling you now that this leap of faith is going to be rewarded in a way that could not have been perceived in the past. Some of you are ready to discover how unlimited you truly are. Humankind is a collective energy of All That Exists in every realm on all worlds everywhere. You are much bigger, broader and grander than you can imagine at this time.

This information is what we are defining in a new way for you. It is coded energetically to reach those of you who might not have understood these words in the past. You may not have connected with the truthfulness of this information or you may have missed the opportunity to receive this knowledge. By allowing yourselves to live this life and to become the Unlimited Resource that you are, you will be a living example to all others.

In the past, living as an Unlimited Resource would have been viewed as a concept or theory since none of you have actually seen this in practice. Jesus the Christed One was living as an Unlimited Resource when on the earth plane. At this time, there are many who are becoming aware of the expanded possibilities available to them. Many are beginning to experience these empowering energies firsthand. What would have appeared to be a miracle in the past, many of you are performing now. You are the living example of this concept as it unfolds on the planet.

Begin each day by meditating on expanding the Eternal Flame that exists in your solar plexus area. This will allow the vibration of your energy to be raised and clear any negative energy you have acquired. You will release any emotional burdens you are carrying, which will re-energize the cells in your physical system. By performing this meditation daily, you will allow your system to be renewed and re-energized.

You have been living under the strains, limitations and structural anomalies acquired through the cellular memories of your family genetics. Through diligence, this can be transmuted and brought back into alignment. This will be visible to all who come in contact with you. As you rejuvenate and regenerate, you will become the Golden light that will draw people to you and to your information.

Many of you are further along with your process than you realize. You have searched long and diligently, wanting connection to this higher aspect of Self. Becoming the God Within is what we are asking you to do. By getting in touch with this energy in the solar plexus, you are tapping into the energetic part of Creator that resides within you. By bringing this energy through the entire body, you are allowing this part of Self to become the largest, strongest part of you. Spiritually and physically, you and your God Self are becoming one. When these energies are blended together, working in function and form with one another, there is nothing you cannot do. The Creator energy within is the creative power source of the universe. It is the fuel that powers all comprehension, all creative energy and all abilities. This is what we are asking you to reconnect to within yourselves. This will allow the God Within to become a part of all you are so you may become All That Is. This is a most glorious time for each of you.

Cecelia: Through this work and through this energy, there is going to be a great awakening. The content behind these words contains energetic coding. The frequencies of the combinations of words, as they are put together, create the power, energy and flow. We are utilizing this method, for we have access to knowledge of those channels in humans that still need the most clearing. This is what these words are designed to do. Now that we are in the new millennium, it is necessary for this to occur.

There is a new world being created by those of you who have been transformed through connection to your expanded Self. Those who would hold the planet in limitation will not be able to grasp this energy to retain their power. The energy is moving the way it must to create a webbing of light and an energy force field around the planet. This protection is being created from within this world, not from without. It is not coming from your extraterrestrial brothers or your Spirit Guides. It is coming from the God Self within each light Worker.

Nancy: Note to Light Workers: If you are reading this material, you are a Light Worker. Light Workers are those conscious of their light, intent on expanding that light and connecting it to others. It is, however, possible to be a light

Worker and not know any of these concepts. Those who come from a place of purity, innocence and love are the most successful Light Workers, for they are not imprisoned by the mind and their energy flows freely from the heart.

After the channeling, we reviewed what had occurred. We were told that the following meditation would anchor the information for those reading this work and help them become part of the Expanded Self. If used daily, the meditation would also help explain the concept of becoming the God Self, which would assist in the transmutation process and allow the encoded information to elevate your vibrations.

The God Spark Meditation

Get into a comfortable position in a chair or on the floor. Affirm your intention to be in a place of peace and calm. The next few minutes are for your expansion, so allow all your worries and cares to slip away. You are now alone in the universe, your only concern being to become as relaxed as possible. Settle in, and become conscious of your breath. See every inhalation bringing light into your entire body and filling you up. On each exhalation, see negativity, darkness and bodily pain leaving. Blow it away from your body for the first six breaths.

Before you begin this exercise, become aware of the light that resides in the center of your solar plexus. As you focus on this light, allow it to glow brighter and stronger and larger. With each inhalation, see the light double in size. Now, focus on both your breathing and on the light until it fills your entire body and auric field.

Continue expanding the light outward from your body to fill the room, the neighborhood, the city, state, country, planet and the universe as you so choose. You decide how far you wish to expand your reach and whom you wish to encounter. It is important to allow whatever area or being shows up to be a part of this expansion.

Allow your expanded light to flow outward and merge with all things. If any discomfort arises, simply disconnect from any energy, entity or place that raises your heart rate. The primary purpose of this meditation is for you to have conscious awareness of the power of your Inner light. It will radiate to such a high degree that you will be able to use it for the transmutation of bodily constrictions, manifestation and the creation of higher frequencies. Your channels will be cleared of debris.

Know that you will have access to all information. Your physical system will be revitalized. Take time to connect to the inner core of light that is your own frequency. Hold this image, *and then see your light expanding and glowing in the colors of white, pink, blue, green and purple. Try on these colors to see how they feel and what their use might be.*

Direct the light or colors to any place in your body that feels pain or blockage. Twirl the light into that area, and see it revitalize. Feel the release of pain. Hold the light energy in that place until the vision of health and wholeness come to your mind. In this way, you are helping to heal your body.

As you feel complete with this process, bring your consciousness gradually back into the room. When you fully return to your present body awareness, open your eyes at will. Allow time to feel relaxation and peace before returning to the tasks of the day. Let this peaceful feeling go with you in all things.

Prayer for Peace and Surrender

In addition to the above meditation, the following prayer will allow you to strengthen your connection to Creator, dispel your past confusion and renew your sense of faith. The pain of the past will be dispersed into the light as you feel at peace once more.

> *Dear God,*
> *Please take me from the pain and emptiness I feel.*
> *Into your hands, I place my future*
> *and all answers yet unknowable to me.*
> *I need only feel your love to know perfection in all things.*
> *Show me my purpose.*
> *Lead me step by step to the place*
> *where my life's work may reveal itself.*
> *Help me surrender to your Divine Plan*
> *that I may know peace.*
> *May I be ever aware of your quiet voice within,*
> *guiding me through the darkness,*
> *explaining that which I cannot comprehend,*
> *assuring me of your constant love.*
> *Amen*

Chapter Thirteen

CREATING YOUR WORLD

The following discourse is further explanation of why the channeling sessions were being given to us. This material, which was channeled through both Nancy and Cecelia, unless otherwise noted, is for all who are ready to receive it and to awaken to the capacity of the expanded Self. The group energy known as the Elohim continues with the following channeled message on the nature of humanity's evolution.

The idea of miracles, Angels and mystical experiences may seem like fictional happenings for heroes in a storybook or merely the delusions of those seriously out of touch with reality. The reason for sharing remarkable stories of Angelic presence, graceful salvation in the moment of Truth and miraculous recovery is that we wish for you to understand that these experiences of the Fifth Dimensional world are obtainable by all. This means that you are all able to transform formerly held belief systems in one instant.

True change is available to all, and you can escape from the ruts of your lives and begin to live fully and purposefully. There can be a sense of wonder and excitement about what's coming next. You can determine what that will be, as you create choices based on a broader expectation, an understanding of the limitless nature of what is possible. As soon as you change your minds, you can change your reality. Thus, miracles occur.

But many of you still feel the unhealed portions of Self that rise up at the dawning of awareness. You have sought solace by hiding under the influence of drugs, alcohol, sex, food, religion or anything else that helps you distance you from your pain. This pain has been seen as the enemy rather than the highlight to your disorder. Often you have felt you were barely holding your life together, when it seemed your arms and legs might fly off in opposite directions.

You have believed in love everlasting, but it has been a fanciful notion, always just out of your grasp. You have searched for love endlessly, looking into the faces of strangers, wondering if one of them might be the one to save you from yourself. You have believed that you have found love again and again when what you actually encountered were people that reflected those parts of Self that longed to be exposed and brought to the light for clearing. Frequently, the process of this clearing didn't feel like love. In many encounters, the kindness and romance faded quickly, leaving the unfaithful parts of Self reflected in the failed relationship.

Anytime you have not been true to Self, you found someone who reflected your negative projection. Anytime you have been true to Self, you also miraculously found someone to carry out that positive projection. You are powerful beyond measure and attract what is needed for your understanding and healing. Betrayal can be extensive and painful. Your belief in love can be shattered again and again until you realize that you must be faithful to Self, that love must first be found within before it can be experienced in the form of relationship to others. It is a difficult journey to Self-discovery, to Truth and, ultimately, back to Creator.

In each one of you there is a child who longs for the wonder of creation, the magic of Christmas and the security and peace of restful sleep. But, if your family of origin suffers from the epidemic of dysfunction, your feelings have been hurt and you have been promised one thing but received another. In time, you learned to protect yourself from a dangerous world.

Merging the incomplete parts of Self may take a long time and bring about many painful experiences before you awaken to the wisdom of the lessons of the Soul. Reading every new book, attending healing retreats and taking classes will not bring you out of the darkness until you realize that your outer experience is a clear reflection of your inner world. You draw to your Self those issues needing to be resolved. The greater your level of denial about who you are, the more profoundly painful will be your experiences. Conversely, the greater Self-acceptance you achieve, the more Truth and beauty you will encounter in your life.

When you are in judgment, you are expressing fear and insecurity about your place in the world. When you are in fear, there is an absence of love. Where love exists, there is no need for judgment. Judgment is the negative charge that binds an emotion or event into your life experience. It holds the event securely in place and casts a shadow over the light you are seeking. As you begin to reclaim your true identity, you will find a new willingness to accept the love vibration. The love vibration gently moves in and begins to release any areas of judgment, hatred and shame. It is through this very love that all healing occurs.

The love vibration has the power to heal those processes that are addictive in nature. Whether the addiction is in the physical, emotional or mental body, addiction requires a focused energy into a substance outside of Self. This disempowerment convolutes spiritual energy and cries for redirection. When you love even those addictions that seem to be most limiting, you are assisting them in moving away from you by releasing the charge they have over you. You know that addictions are limiting in nature, but you encourage love of any process that shows you your resistance to opening to love. There are those of you who can only love that which is outside your Self—be it an animal, a drug or another human being. You have not yet seen the beauty and perfection of the Soul that lives within. As you love your addiction, that love can remove the emotional and constrictual charge it causes.

Nearly everyone is addicted in some way to something. It can be a habit, a process or a chemical. We ask you to understand that the love of a particular thing will open the gates and expand the possibility of a future love in larger and more numerous ways. How frequently have you heard of someone who put down a particular addiction only to take up another one? It is your judgment surrounding the addiction, questioning whether you should or should not indulge in your habit, that keeps you in constant conflict and rigidity. It is as if the box gets moved from one place to the other, but all the while you are still in the box.

We want to clarify the need for expanding the thought process away from judgment and into acceptance. This is true no matter what is happening in your life, on your path or in your choices. All choices are for the highest good at the time they are chosen, whether or not it may seem so at the time.

How often have you looked upon the path you have taken and said, "If only..." or "What if..."? It was the choice taken, the road chosen, and it was absolutely perfect for where you were at that time in your life. You chose what needed to be looked at and what needed to be encountered. Often, you dismissed the experience after understanding that the clothing didn't fit, that the shoe wasn't your size or the road was not to your liking. But every path you choose to explore, even momentarily, is one of advantage and gain. Each experience is educational at best and exhausting at worst, but each is weaving the tapestry of your Soul as it continues onward.

It has been said, "There is nothing more than love," "Love is all there is" and "Love is all." We would ask you again to turn inward with love and to understand that all places within your Soul are there for love and for purpose. If you could turn inward with love and release Self-judgment, there would occur an immediate and radical physical, mental and emotional healing.

When you are moving forward on your path and your progress is at a pinnacle, you often feel your foundations being shaken. There is a place within you that may still feel unworthy and undeserving to be in a place of grandeur, joy and well-being. But if you feel no Self Love, you can't recognize your own worth. You may, on some deep level, have the fear that the changes you are making are a dream or an illusion. You may be afraid you will be disappointed in what you have dared to believe possible for you. You may see a bright, shining beacon in front of you—always just out of reach.

You have all begun new relationships, basking in their glow. In them, you were filled with hope, joy and love. You felt wonderful about yourself. But as the relationship progressed, you allowed the judgments and interferences of the world to disrupt what was once beautiful. These painful areas of learning are necessary for each and every one of you. Each relationship has been about uncovering the next layer. It has been about removing old blocks, unresolved issues and negative vibrations that you have carried since the beginning.

Cecelia: *You do not enter into this world a blank slate. Each one of you comes in with the chemical imprinting and genetic coding from all those generations that have come before you. The body forms itself around your Soul vibration and the vibrations of your human lineage. You are traveling in a vehicle that has been co-created by your Soul and the genetics of your extended earth family. Most of you are unaware that the generational issues you leave unresolved will resurface to be cleared by those who come after you. The unresolved issues of your ancestors have influenced your life's experience.*

You may wonder how you can undo what has taken many thousands of lifetimes to create. We want to reemphasize that this is do-able within a few moments of time. It only requires allowing the love that you are to express itself. By accepting the God Spark within, you can finally understand yourself at the deepest levels of your body, mind and Spirit. You can free your body by allowing Self-judgment to be cleared by the love vibration.

By accepting the light within you, your Soul can be transmuted in a twinkling of an eye. A Soul-level adjustment allows realignment between your Spirit and your physical body. The alignment of your spinal column is a direct reflection of where you are out of alignment with your God Spark, your true Self. You have allowed, and agreed to, whatever is occurring now in order to bring this information forward. You are being given the opportunity to move through this in a very rapid way. You are going to understand that you are now at the place and time to realign Divine Will with the Will of Self. This alignment of wills allows your Soul to operate freely throughout your body, free of interference. You will receive the assistance of those Angels and Guides around you that are here to celebrate and enhance this occurrence.

It is a rare thing when those of you in the physical have taken this giant step. When this occurs, there are many present to witness and assist in the releasing of your body's last attempt to hold on to old programming. This is not a statement that should cause any judgment about how well you are doing spiritually. The alignment of the wills with the Soul creates a final clearing. This allows the next level of spiritual evolution. Your body is cleared to allow your deeper spiritual nature to shine through. This is a wondrous thing, for you are being released in a way that you would not have believed possible in the past.

Self-Judgment Release Affirmations

I RELEASE MYSELF FROM THE NEED
TO JUDGE
OTHERS OR MYSELF.

I OPEN MYSELF TO RECEIVE THE
LOVE VIBRATION AS IT FLOWS IN
FROM CREATOR.

I ACCEPT THAT CREATOR DOES NOT
JUDGE ME.

THOUGH MANY THINGS ARE
UNKNOWABLE TO ME,

I TRUST THAT CREATOR IS
DIRECTING MY PATH.

Prayer for Release and Empowerment

The following prayer assists in the encoded release of those people and events from our pasts that still hold a negative charge, even as we realize that these people and events have been necessary for the evolution of our Souls' growth.

Dear God,

I am eternally grateful

for the Exquisite Beings who have brought to me

the wounded pieces of my self for healing.

Although the pain was deep, I know it was required

for this level of healing.

Without the intensity of these experiences,

I surely would have faltered longer on the path of

shadows,

darkness and illusion.

I pray that my learning will be graceful and move

quickly.

It is my desire and intent to have

a glorious, joyous life in which to play,

where all needs, desires and wishes are fulfilled.

Let there be no more need for struggle or concern.

May all of my energies now manifest heaven on

earth.

I accept that I am the co-creator of my life

experience,

and that all things are possible with Your help.

Amen.

Chapter Fourteen

EXPANDING
THE LIGHT

Channeling continues with the group energy known as the Elohim. Nancy is the receiver, and Cecelia is holding the energy of light and compassion for these Divine transmissions to come through. We find that The Teachings consistently seek to find the deepest part of the sleeping Self, to awaken it into the full consciousness of illumined Soul awareness.

There lies within each one of you an essence of light, the energy of Infinite Creation, love and awareness. This Inner light is the aspect of Creator that inhabits all things. It is your precious, inalienable connection to the One, to All There Is. As you become aware of this light and begin to work with acknowledging and expanding its properties, you are mystically reawakened to the power of your own God Self as it readies to reclaim its connection with the One.

When re-ignited, the light Within will allow your body to be released from old patterns. It becomes a transmuting flame that clears all the cells of your body and seeks to find any areas of darkness or limitation that are still being held in your cellular memory. This spiritual energy searches out all systems of the body and releases physical and generational sources of limitation. This clearing is a natural occurrence when you consciously work with the Inner Flame every day. This is the quickest way to expose those aspects of Self that have been hiding from your most diligent healing processes. Once this light has been consciously expanded, there is nothing that can hide from the Creator within.

As you set yourself free from the limitations of the past acquired through multiple lifetimes, you begin to recognize the limitless nature of your own Spirit. By allowing the power of your light to shine through, others can connect with your God Spark energy.

All family members carry similar cellular structure and genetic coding. This creates the potential for clearing many generations at one time. As you expand the light within, it filters throughout your entire system. From there, it can spread its energy to those around you and beyond, spreading outward into the universe.

What affects you affects all other things. You are part of All There Is. By healing yourself, you are helping heal all other things. As you are healed, others interacting with you and seeing your transformation may become open to their own process. Your energy has the power to become a catalyst for the Inner Flame within others. Exposure to your expanded light energy can facilitate a clearing and energy up-grade in others. The energy that flows through you is compatible with the God Spark in everyone. It is all the same energy.

As you begin to feel the expansion of your own light, you may experience warmth or hear a sound in the center of your head. There may be a feeling of energy running throughout your body, an inner vision or a knowing that a force within you is expanding through every cell of your body. Your life force will become stronger and brighter, and you will feel yourself being energized from within. It will create a vibration within your cellular structure that can release all remnants of past imprinting that is no longer appropriate for you. When the energy channels are clear, the vibration can move back and forth between the chakras and meridians, free of interference.

Visualization, when combined with the power of the Inner Flame meditation, is one of the strongest combinations that can be used to enhance your co-creative energy. As you move into your own power, you can decide how to best use your new creative energy. You will be ready to decide what projects will most enhance your new level of connection to the needs of your Soul.

We received the following channeled message that explains the process of co-creation.

Decide what you want. See how it feels when you visualize yourself in a certain situation or with a certain person.

Set your intention to co-create. Commit to becoming that which is now in your grasp. Do not consider failure as an option.

Imagine your Self in the midst of your new project. You are smiling, energized and expanded. You are powerful, and others are reaping the rewards of your generosity and Spirit.

See, feel and vibrate to the frequencies of successful co-creation. You are moving into your potential as a Universal Creator, working with the Unlimited Resources of All There Is.

The process of co-creation often requires a willingness to explore the limitations that have held you back in the past. By utilizing the power of the Inner Flame, all your limitations and old programming can be transmuted from the cellular structure in a moment. This creates the spiritual hygiene that allows you to know your true feelings. You begin to allow yourself to feel what you truly want. The heart, your feeling center, is always involved when you bring anything into creation, intended or not.

Get in touch with your heart center and allow its desires to come into your consciousness. Then speak the words that bring what you want into form. Positive projection does precede the creation of form. It is important that your intention is spoken out loud. This allows the universe to hear very clearly what you want. The heart center provides the feeling that ignites the intention. You need to look at the intention as if it is the Inner

Flame itself. Putting your intention out there with feeling and emotion fuels the flame into existence. When the feeling center is fully engaged and your intention is clear, you can manifest your heart's desire into physical reality.

It is within your power to bring your intentions into solid form when your feeling center is behind it. It is important to clear the heart center by opening yourself to feelings you have hidden from yourself. You must allow yourself to become vulnerable to your own emotions. Your greatest strength lies in knowing how you feel about what you are saying and doing. This is the easiest way for you to come into your full power.

We communicate to you through your feeling center as well as through your conscious mind. But your conscious mind, when used to the exclusion of emotions, interferes with your ability to receive our messages. Spirit operates through the heart center with cooperation from the mind. Spirit continuously sends messages to help you gain insight into many areas of your life. By using the God Spark meditation, you can become aware of discordant energies and take the necessary steps to bring them back into alignment. You may also call on your Guides, your Guardian Angels and us. We are here for you, and our greatest desire is to assist you in moving into clarity, attunement and creation.

Light Within Affirmations

I FREELY OPEN MYSELF TO RECEIVE
THE BLESSINGS OF
ALL THERE IS.

I AM A DIVINE REFLECTION OF THE
GOD SPARK
AS IT IGNITES WITHIN ME.

I ALLOW THE POWER OF MY SPIRIT
TO BENEFIT ALL OTHERS AND
MYSELF.

MY REALITY IS A REFLECTION OF THE
STATE
OF MY OWN SPIRIT.

Chapter Fifteen

LESSONS FOR THE SOUL

The following information was channeled through Nancy:

It has often been said that the apple doesn't fall far from the tree. When this interpretation is applied to families, it typically creates an angry reaction. Few of you are happy with both parents and fewer still wish to claim similarities to either of them. Most of you prefer to focus on the negative aspects of your parents and family members rather than accept your rightful inheritance. This continues until the magic of spiritual maturity occurs, bringing you understanding and acceptance for those who conceived you, forgiving them their humanity and embracing their positive qualities.

It is at this time of true adulthood that you begin to forgive yourself, releasing blame and assuming personal responsibility. What matters at this time is making the most of what you learned from your experiences. All lessons of family life are put in your path for the purpose of teaching, typically through contrast, that which your Soul needs for its greater expansion, evolution and growth.

To deny your parents is to deny Self. You have inherited their genes, their opinions and emotional makeup, their physiological addictions and their denial of Spirit within. You share their gifts as well as their blocks to eventual expansion and Soul growth. The family you are born into provides the perfect opportunity to strengthen those aspects of your Soul that yearn for expression and understanding. It is a cosmic gift of your own choosing that has brought you to your family situation in order to master love for Self and others.

Your family of origin has given you the blueprint for the healing of your Soul. By the age of 30, this has often shifted in a very broad way. Though many tragedies may occur before then that are unfortunate for your heart's sake, they help create a willingness to move into a broader scope of perception. This is significant for your understanding of what humanity must go through in order to heal the wounds of the generations that came before and the ones that will come after.

To disclaim honor to either of your parents is to go against Creator: You cannot honor your Self if you do not honor your parents. You cannot be in judgment of the imperfections of your parents' bloodlines and still look kindly upon yourself.

It is Universal Law to love and honor the Self within as a reflection of Creator Source. You and your parents chose to be born into your family for the lessons that were needed to heal at the Soul level. By honoring the reflection of your parents in yourself, you allow your heart to heal. This is the quickest and most loving path to follow on your journey Home. Love each of them in yourself as intently as you love your friends and your life mates. For truly, the one you will be honoring is the God Self that exists in each of you.

It is also your responsibility to honor your body as the housing for Creator within. The only real reason to have your earthly body is to have a vessel for Soul to do its work on this earth plane.

We would have you picture an army of people lined up in rows. In the front row are your children, in the second row are your grandchildren and in the third row are your great grandchildren—and so on down the line. Among these familiar faces you also see many that belong to your friends, business associates and even perceived enemies—all together in the group you now call family.

Each and every one of you is filled with criticism and judgment of the actions and behaviors of others in your family. These judgments create in you feelings of superiority.

Judgment has been the single greatest struggle of humanity. This is true whether you are healing and growing through your youth or whether you are old enough to have made all the mistakes made by your own mother and father. Each of you will add your own missteps to the collective consciousness. One day, you will realize that judgment is a waste of your energy and has tied you to the very energies you are judging. Whether you focus your energy on joy or on sorrow, it will become stronger within you.

Judgment begins within your own family, takes root within your heart and moves outward into the world. Conversely, love and forgiveness will heal your heart, your family relationships and radiate out into the world as a powerful force for healing.

As you commit yourself to releasing judgment and to honoring your father and mother, you can connect to the love that resides within you and pass it along to future generations. Loving this blended energy inside yourself is the greatest gift you can give your children.

In this moment, healing is occurring for those of you who are seeking spiritual enlightenment, for enlightenment is where light shines into the darkened recesses of Self. You are truly allowing this to occur as we give you this message. You have longed for this information to give you Knowing. You have longed for fullness and completion within. You have always prayed to someone or something outside of yourself; in this moment of recognition, you acknowledge the power of praying inward.

As you reflect on your Self and the characteristics of both your parents, you reflect different aspects of Self. As you have judged your siblings for their differences from you, know that those differences are there for your reflection, enlightenment and healing. As siblings, you share similar issues and backgrounds, which allows you to assist one another. Through your own healing and energy upgrade, you are able to share these gifts with your family members.

This understanding is a perfect example of the gift that healing through your pain can bring. Those who attempt to avoid pain also miss the gifts that come from it. You cannot analyze pain or explain it away through your consciousness if you are holding it in your heart. Your heart will not release pain until its true message has been understood. Traditionally, pain has been experienced as a feeling of discomfort in body, mind or Spirit. But you may have failed to recognize its potential for showing you those parts of Self that need to be healed. Pain can be a beacon of light sounding to you. Please honor your pain as an information source, and allow it to flow through you for release.

If you hide from your feelings—whether physical, mental or emotional—you cannot access the guidance that comes from allowing the pain to be followed to its source. By evolving through your pain and its processes, you will receive its gifts. Transmuting through your pain can create an outcome far grander than any you have known.

Your healing will come through accessing the power of the God Self within. Denying or blocking pain will intensify its effects. By understanding your pain and releasing its source, your light will fill the void with the healing power of love. The light within is the energy that heals all darkness, all constrictions, all pain and all generational issues. This light can become a beacon for others who are ready to be healed. The shining forth of this light into the world allows the true healing of your planet to occur.

Through healing the mother-father duality of the earth plane, you reactivate the Divine love that resides within. Divine love is the energy that unites our Inner Male and Inner Female with the co-creative power of

Spirit. Energetically speaking, it is through the merging and blending of these aspects that you heal body, mind and Spirit. This healing honors the God Self within—God, Goddess and All There Is.

Judgment is the greatest Creator of disease and pain within the body. Honor your mother and father in this lifetime by releasing judgment of how they have handled their lives. Let go of how you might have done it better or differently. Allow yourself to move into a place of balance, peace and flow. You have made life choices based on your childhood dreams and on many life experiences and situations you have drawn to your Self for learning.

All experience has been initiated at the Soul level by your deep desire to be healed. You have prayed for healing, balance and Illumination and have resented pain when it was sent as a teacher. Rather than seeing pain as an opportunity to heal your problem, you have seen it as a burden cast upon you. Therefore, you mask the pain with outside medications and chemicals instead of listening to its message—or you look for natural plant products to take the place of learning and transformation. This keeps you moving a little longer in a backward direction until you get to the true source of the illness within.

Illness is a lack of integration that holds us in limitation and creates dark spaces within. We are telling you today that the greatest natural physician on the planet is your Self. The highest form of healing comes from releasing the energy of judgment.

Understand that you chose to enter physicality to heal your Soul and release all attachment to old energy. You are here to be united with the power of your own Spirit and become a conscious co-creator on this planet. You are here to construct a bridge between all disconnected aspects of Self. Now is the time for this construction to begin. You can thank your parents for agreeing to allow you this opportunity to rediscover your true Self.

Soul Lesson Affirmations

I HONOR MY BODY AS THE TEMPLE OF
THE CREATOR WITHIN.

I LOVE AND HONOR MY PARENTS AS
MY GREATEST TEACHERS.

I APPRECIATE THE LEARNING FROM
MY FAMILY OF ORIGIN.

I RECOGNIZE AND HONOR THE
SACRIFICES OF THE GENERATIONS
THAT HAVE COME BEFORE ME.

Prayer for Honoring Parents

Dear God,

Today, I begin to integrate the love of my parents deep within.

I ask to be at peace with my origins.

In the deepest recesses of my memory,

I will access and confirm that I truly chose

my mother and my father for the perfect beings they are.

I know my soul longed for that which only they could give me.

I fully honor their influence on my life, now and forever.

I take responsibility for knowing I did choose to transmute,

not to judge, the frailties my parents had yet to overcome.

My soul knew I could learn from their exquisite humanness.

I call forth Angels who light my way as I transmute these energies.

Allow me to understand more fully that my soul's growth

brought about incidents of pain, neglect and lack

so I would have the opportunity to heal my family's darkness.

I call forth the unhealed portions of self

for the illumination and healing of my soul.

I fully accept the integration of all that I am

that I may be the reflection of healed spiritual light for myself,

for my children and for all who I may encounter.

Amen.

Chapter Sixteen

THE POWER
OF INTENTION

Those of us with conscience, love and the desire to grow and assist others frequently misunderstand the energy of abundance and material wealth. But it is entirely within our birthright in this material world to express ourselves through material means.

Nancy and Cecelia received the following channeled message:

Remember the parable, The Eye of the Needle, from the book of Matthew in the Bible. Jesus is quoted as saying, "How hard it will be for those who have riches to enter the kingdom of God...It is easier for a camel to go through the Eye of the Needle than for a rich man to enter the kingdom of God." This is often interpreted to mean that material wealth should not be a spiritual goal. This is not true.

More than 2,000 years ago, traveling merchants in the Middle East hastened their trade journeys by passing through a natural, extremely narrow valley of stone called the Eye of the Needle. This path was so narrow that only a camel without baggage could find its way through. This meant that before passing through this barrier, merchants had to unload their goods from the camels, guide the animals through the passage and then reload the goods after safe passage.

A rich man with cumbersome material possessions had a difficult time getting through the Eye of the Needle. This did not mean he had to abandon his possessions and impoverish himself, but it did require him to relinquish them temporarily. For a wealthy man to leave his possessions, even temporarily, suggested he had faith that transcended material things.

Today, being willing to release whatever possessions you find necessary in order to pass through this life journey smoothly is very different from the notion that having wealth is evil. Money, gold and silver do not carry negative vibrations. It is only when they become part of an overriding sense of greed and possessiveness that they become tools of manipulation.

There is much joy to be found in beauty, cleanliness and order. Indeed, the outer world of your creation— your houses, your offices, your cars and your workspaces—is a perfect mirror of your inner world. When you have accepted your power, your love and the perfection of your path, you allow the universe to send all manner of riches into your world. It is when you deem yourselves worthy that abundance flows to you with ease, allowing you to focus your attention on creativity and joy and away from the vibration of fear and lack.

You need to balance giving and receiving in your lives so that Spirit may manifest bountifully.

There is a poverty consciousness that has developed around spirituality that originated with the beginnings of Christianity. Those religious figures that came after Jesus the Christed One taught early Christians that material possessions and wealth were evil in order to control the wealth themselves. This has contributed to your deeply held belief that a rich man cannot be spiritual and a religious man cannot be rich. These beliefs have been passed down to you through cellular memory, your genetic history, your culture and planetary consciousness. They have contributed to locking your species into servitude, struggle and oppression.

These cellular beliefs continue to affect many seekers on the path to enlightenment. It is time for you to shift this awareness for a clearer understanding of what it means to be spiritual and successful in the material world.

There are those of you who ask, "Who will provide for me if I am on my spiritual path? Who will see to my earthly needs?" It is important that you realize that Spirit is what you are, not a destination outside Self. Care of your spiritual Self requires a certain level of physical awareness and acceptance— awareness of what your needs are and acceptance of the reality of your situation—to determine what you would like to create differently. You may hold great interest in acquisition or you may choose to live simply, owning few material possessions. Either way, the choice and the responsibility are yours.

For many of you, the choice depends on whether you feel you deserve to have what you want. For others, the choice is more basic—deciding what you want.

When you consider the foundation of your reality as a joint venture between Spirit and Consciousness, you may begin to consider how much materiality you desire. Focusing on the material will produce more of the same. Dwelling on Spirit will enhance the comfort of being at Home within. The balancing factor is intent: Your desire to have and to hold, to love and be loved or to achieve great worldly wealth and recognition, is set in motion by your intention. These are the choices of your Soul.

This choice has nothing to do with judgment or superiority. It has to do with what is needed for your present level of Soul expression. Ultimately, the Soul seeks balance in all things, gracefully flowing through physical density at will, creating and manifesting instantaneously what is required in the moment.

You need to seek clarity of purpose so you can decide just what you wish to create. You need to do this knowing that your spiritual nature is reflected in your life's work and every chosen activity. You must rely on your own independent Spirit to move forward. What may seem insignificant today may reveal something momentous in the future. As your inner promptings lead you to make new decisions, that energy propels you toward your future. Projecting your focused energy on a goal with clear intent will bring you all that resonates with that energy. In this way, your consciousness expands the vibration of abundance and attraction.

Clarity of purpose and intention are the No. 1 and No. 2 elements necessary to attract the abundance you desire. You create with every thought and emotion, so you are either creating consciously or unconsciously. It is important to engage your conscious awareness in positive thought forms that will assist positive manifestation.

As you think, so you become. Resistance to change and reluctance to flow with your own spiritual nature mire your progression in a vortex of quicksand. The more resistance, the greater your downward spiral until, finally, there is nothing to do but give in to what Spirit needs. You have a propensity to stay in one place too long. When the breath of life has gone from a situation or a relationship, you often continue to cling to them for dear life, which is like attempting to breathe life into a corpse. But, the remedy is to let go. As energy is freed, it transforms itself into its most usable form once again.

You may feel suffocated when you hold too tightly to something that no longer has meaning in your life. Only by remaining open to change can you feel true growth and success. So you need to decide what you want and maintain that thought with clear focus and intention. Allow Spirit to direct your activities, always embracing change and surrendering to your Inner Guidance.

You must love the Truth of what you are doing to such a high degree that the love of that activity alone would suffice.

You cannot be separated from that which is always in you. At times, you have felt abandoned by Creator, but from the perspective of Spirit, it is always you who have abandoned Creator, for Creator has always been part of who you are. But you usually choose to recognize everything outside of yourself before turning within and realizing that the Source, the Unlimited Resource, for everything you seek is within you.

You should never seek remedies for your life situation through the efforts of others. The true remedies reside within as a direct result of accessing your Truth through contemplation, meditation and peaceful surrender while taking the next step to move through your own resistance.

The God Within attempts to communicate every moment with the beings you are. You are constantly being sent feelings, messages of the heart, yet you turn away from your heart and allow outside influences to be more important. It is only by having the courage to break free from outside influences, in spite of any fear you might experience, that you change your course of action and change your life path. Fear of the unknown was created in early human history when going into an unknown place with potential predators might cost you your life. On some level, you still struggle with this today. But you should not revile that fear when you feel it; it is not an unwanted companion. It is an indication that your life is moving forward, that you are being released from your past. After this release, you can begin to feel the vibrations of your True essence.

When the God Within is Self aware, there is no room for fear because you have access to all information necessary. Your feet will be guided down the correct path. You will walk surely and clearly forward, resonating in tune with yourself, your world and the universe. Know that you experience all things as part of the learning process.

Each one of you possesses the power to make a difference and the power to create change. It is the intention through which you deliver words, energy, feelings and emotions that creates a powerful reaction. When you are clear in your purpose and intent, you become a powerful co-creator. Clarity and intention allows you to establish yourself in a grounded way. It eliminates all fear and anxiety and allows you to develop the strength and stamina needed to move you forward with purpose.

You need to hold these thoughts close to your heart, and remember to maintain a place of equilibrium as things around you shift and change. These messages carry the codes of transmutation that will uplift you and carry you Home.

Chapter Seventeen

THE OPEN HEART

According to Universal Law, when we ask, we receive. In learning to receive, however, it is first necessary to open our hearts and feel what Inner Guidance is telling us. Many of us feel more comfortable with the workings of the intellect rather than following the dictates of our hearts. It is not easy to find ourselves in painful emotional situations that feel like errors in judgment. But it is from these very painful situations that our next level of learning is revealed. It is from open and loving hearts communing with the Spirit inhabiting our physical bodies, that we learn to become our Higher Selves.

Both Nancy and Cecelia received the following channeled message:

In popular metaphysical lore, denying yourself a need is the surest way to obtain it. Admitting need perpetuates the condition of needing. So how can you sort out the feelings, fears and anxieties you have about getting your needs met?

According to this metaphysical philosophy, you need to claim what you already have in Spirit even though it is not currently available in your physical reality. But when you have an open heart, you can allow love to flow into all areas of lack as Spirit fulfills the need.

When you need something, it helps you recognize what particular area of your life seeks more light. Allowing that light to flow into a need, a feeling or a situation creates healing. When you pour openhearted love into all things, it aids the co-creative process of abundance.

Masters, mystics and sages have achieved a state of perpetual bliss that requires nothing, but for the majority of you in the material world, there is still the issue of requirement. For the Masters who find exquisite joy and peace in all things, their calm center is not dependent on outer circumstance but on peaceful acceptance of the perfection of all things. They know that the Divine provides all things. When you tap into this power of bliss in the eternal Now, in full appreciation of each moment, your true creative power magnifies.

Your Inner Guidance, the wisdom of your heart and the longing of your Soul are constantly sending messages to your conscious mind about when you feel full and when you do not. One way your Soul speaks to you is through the feeling of need. When you need food, your body signals you that you are hungry, so you seek food. By allowing yourself to identify without judgment what you need, you give yourself permission to have those needs fulfilled. You automatically begin to resonate with a vibration that calls forth the missing piece: "I am now ready for Spirit to enter!" By accepting, without desperation, the condition of lack and assuming your needs will be met in a timely manner, you release the negative charge of need and create space to receive from the universe. An open heart allows all to flow freely.

Consider the needs of newborn babies. When wet, cold or hungry, they cry out. There is no holding back for fear that the universe will not fulfill their needs. If the child's mother, or a surrogate, is nearby, she will do what she can to fulfill what is needed. In this way, the mother acts as the earthly presence of God for all of us. She is there to love, protect and provide for the needs of her creation. By being like a newborn babe, you release your fear that your needs will not be met or that you don't deserve to have them met. By accepting your needs and expecting them to be met, they will be.

As you mature, you inevitably meet with disappointment. It is a shock for little ones to find restrictions on their free expression. The farther you move from this early pure state of Spirit, the more you forget your Inner Guidance and your true identity. The less you accept your Inner Knowing, the more you draw to you experiences that do not accept your Inner Knowing. The more disappointment you feel, the more you draw to you experiences that are disappointing. Gradually, you lose your sense of personal power. Instead, you accept what comes.

Feelings are your way Home. They are guideposts, beacons of light illuminating your path, messages from Spirit. Whether you feel safe, frightened, angry, and blissful or in a state of love, you are being guided. The expansion or the compression you feel in your heart is Creator within. When your heart feels expanded, Spirit approves of the reason why. If your heart feels restricted, Spirit does not approve. By listening to your feelings, by noting what expands or compresses your energy, you can discover what you are being led to do, whether it is completing a task or releasing a pattern in order to free your energetic flow.

By following your passions, you learn to create from a place of joy—a place full of the acknowledgement of who you are. This is the source of the Empowered Beings of light, living in the Spirit of Creator on this earthly plane of existence.

When you feel pain, you feel you have made poor choices, which causes you to distrust your feelings. You do not need to distrust. Instead, you need to realize that through your feelings you are drawn to experiences you need for the growth of your Soul. These feelings may be painful. Your life may be turned completely upside down by the results of a relationship in ruin or a business situation that ended in betrayal. It may feel as if your entire world is collapsing, with only yourself to blame. In retrospect, painful experiences can quite literally take you into your next level of Soul awareness that will help take you Home.

The issue of need around relationships seems to be particularly difficult for you. You may meet someone who heightens your senses, and, having felt particularly flat prior to this meeting, you may be eager to jump into the fray. As the relationship progresses, you may begin to find fault with your partner's philosophies, personal habits or need for your time. As the bliss begins to fade, and you are left with the distinct feeling that you have been misled by your feelings, you realize that you should have run away from the relationship at the first flutter of feeling. Whenever you are drawn to another, you are drawn to missing pieces of Self. Whatever disguise the other may have, this person is showing you the hidden treasures you need to rediscover your Self.

In ancient cultures, romance was considered foolish and irrational. Yet today, a good love story is a safe way to access your feeling center. Today, the romance-novel genre of publications outsells any classic work, fictional best-selling book or academic publication. Most of you are seeking a love connection with your true self. You desire to be reunited with the vibration of your twin flame as a way to reconnect to source. You seem to long for an ecstatic reunion with Spirit, a reunion that has kept you moving forward through many lifetimes of disappointment and disillusionment. You are now at the end of this journey. It is time for these energies to be reunited.

What is there in duality—black and white, day and night—that hasn't been explored? What is left for you as humans to experience? In actuality, we are all energetically One—one energy, one consciousness. We have access to All There Is, to every experience and every lesson that has ever been learned. But the time for gathering duality information is over. It is time to return to who and what you truly are. It is time for the twin flame energies to be reunited on the earth plane. It is time for the love vibration to be expanded on your planet so it can lead you Home. This has been the Divine Plan from the beginning—for love to lead you Home.

Mastery requires desire. Desire requires emotion. Emotion requires identifying a need.

Mastery requires clear identification of which desires, emotions and needs are asking to be addressed. As humans, you tend to subject your own needs to the approval and the judgments of others. You worry that having needs, and acknowledging what they are, opens you to criticism. This is why so many of you find it difficult to know what you need or want; therefore, you destroy your own creativity, feeling that there is nothing to reach out to—or for. If you have never recognized your need for a positive, creative relationship with Self, it cannot happen between you and another.

As you have moved through the tunnel of life and discovered the hidden passageways, we have been with you. As you have called out in pain, we have been with you. As you have wept for loves lost and hopes unrealized, we have been with you, waiting. Waiting to be asked, "Are you there? Will you help me?" The answer always has been, and always will be, "We are with You, Loved Ones. We will help."

So often we have wept for the pain and suffering that was not quieted by our gentle care. You have been reluctant in your pride and in your anger to allow us into your hearts. We have stood in your doorway, waiting to be noticed. We have tapped you on the shoulder to tell you we are here. So many times, you were doubtful of our love and care. So many hearts have been afraid to open to our light. So many of you have been reluctant to have your scars, created through millennia of lifetimes, transmuted by the love vibration that flows from the Source. So many of you have kept us, your spiritual family, from our earthly relations. For you have a grander family than you know. We have been eagerly awaiting the opportunity to be asked back into your lives and your consciousness. How hopeful we have been for the great dance of reunion to begin. We wish to come to you, Dear Ones, bearing gifts of the Spirit, nourishment for your Soul and companions of destiny for you, our brothers and sisters in the flesh.

It is time for you to understand the treasures we are offering you at this precise moment in the history of your Souls' long journey. You have diligently pursued matters of the heart against all seeming defeats, and we applaud you. You have persevered despite all obstacles laid at your feet. Somehow, you have found the strength to pick up your feet and climb across one wall, and then another, until you found the road that is leading you Home. Throughout your journey, we have placed the markers that led you out of darkness.

We have held you as you were sleeping, in loving arms of protection, to allow you a few moments of safety in which you could heal. We have uttered a kind word in your lowest moments to restore your faith. And, yes, we have even walked up to you on the street and greeted you with a smile to brighten your day.

In so many ways, large and small, we have been at your side, offering the peace of the Spirit to our earthly warriors. We are here to tell you that for each misstep you have taken, there were three steps that moved you onward—for every detour encountered, there was a side benefit created and obtained.

We are here now, offering our loving hands to each one of you in a more direct manner. We want you to know that when you ask for our help, we will do all that is allowed to help relieve your burdens. We have longed to do so, but we were not permitted to because of your Will. This is Universal Law: "Thy Will be done." We can only offer our help to those of you who are ready to receive it. There are still so many of you who feel you are not worthy of our intervention. But, we say to you that there has never been a time we would not help you. Like a loving parent, we would watch over you and keep you safe, all the while allowing you freedom to choose your own way.

We are nearing the end of a great cycle in the days of man. You are nearing the graduation day you have long anticipated. There is no longer any need for you to carry the burdens of many lifetimes upon your shoulders. Allow us to assist in your release process. Be very clear about those aspects of Self that are no longer appropriate for your journey.

State your heartfelt desire out loud, and let the universe know you are ready to return to the place of peace and beauty that has been there for you all along. Ask to access your higher faculties of consciousness, and use this energy to make the world a better place for yourself and others.

Dream into creation what your heart desires, and share your vision with others of like mind. Become part of a powerful network of transformation on the planet, and never fail to speak your Truth from a place of love. Release yourself to access the Inner Wisdom that is with you always.

Speak to us often, and share your plans. We long to hear your words and to offer you the gentle nudges that promote a positive outcome for your hearts' desires.

Ask, and it shall be given unto you. Seek, and ye shall find. Knock, and the door shall be opened.

Lord's Prayer

The following prayer carries encoded messages. The repetition of this prayer, which has been translated from Aramaic to English, allows you to receive the vibrational upgrade intended by this material. Write it down, and pray it often. See what comes to you in reverence and surrender to the cosmic forces of Divine nature

> *O, Cosmic Birther of all radiance and vibration,*
>
> *soften the ground of our being, and carve*
>
> *out a space within us where your Presence can abide.*
>
> *Fill us with your creativity so that we may be empowered*
>
> *to bear the fruit of Your mission.*
>
> *Let each of our actions bear fruit in accordance with our desire.*
>
> *Endow us with the wisdom to produce*
>
> *what we need to grow and flourish.*
>
> *Untie the tangled threads of destiny that bind us*
>
> *as we release others from the entanglement of past mistakes.*
>
> *Do not let us be seduced by that which would divert us*
>
> *from our true purpose,*
>
> *but illuminate the opportunities of the present moment.*
>
> *For You are the ground and the fruitful vision,*
>
> *the birth, power and fulfillment,*
>
> *as all is gathered and made whole once again.*
>
> *Amen.*

Chapter Eighteen

RETURNING HOME

The following channeled discourse on returning Home and the union of twin flame Souls continues through Nancy:

Nancy: The only energy capable of removing negative imprinting is love. Love comes through the release of fear through the vibration of forgiveness of Self and others. Feeling love and compassion for all and speaking from your heart in honesty, integrity and balance helps release a negative charge around any issue, allowing the creation of a new beginning.

On this earthly sojourn, you experience much in the way of duality. You must experience the high and low, the in and out, the up and the down, for it is in this manner of seeking contrast that you learn and grow. If you have not experienced cruelty, you cannot appreciate kindness. If you have not known weakness, how can you know strength? It is time to understand that there is no right or wrong, only experiences expressing themselves in duality.

The most difficult forgiveness is forgiveness of Self. There is great power in the spiritual act of forgiveness and release, both of Self and others. It allows you to let go of experiences that have locked you into a place of fear and distrust and into the illusion that you were not safe. Speak words of forgiveness as they come, allowing them to flow from your heart. Their energies will allow your vibration to shift and penetrate into the very core of your being. Releasing these blocked energies will help release your feeling of loneliness and separation. In this illusion of separation, you have had great fear of not being accepted. This negative vibration held in your Soul has kept you from expressing your feelings and has invalidated your sense of Self. It is now time to speak up, knowing that you are loved, safe and understood. For in so doing, you encourage others to do the same. By bringing this information into relationship, both of you may heal and become whole in your full life expression. There is no better place to upgrade the core Self than through the eyes of intimacy. Venture into life's most promising adventure, into the sharing of life with another Soul and find your way Home.

Often you have hidden in relationships that are undemanding, with those whose eyes cannot see into your Soul. You were not ready to see our Truth or to compassionately deal with the growth of another. For that time of holding back, we now say it is time to flow forward into your own future of love, light and the embraces of the Soul that are so pure and strong you will never look back. If a relationship calls, allow your heart to expand with possibility. Heed the call. Pick up the challenge, and move ahead.

Feel the Truth within, and utilize the power of your Spirit to dissolve all energies that are holding you back or creating fear. Pick up your sword, and be brave. Become your own knight in shining armor. It is time for women and men alike to take on the role of the Spiritual Warrior.

The Spiritual Warrior is always aware of who and what they allow to enter into their field of influence. They impartially exclude all energy that would interfere with moving Self and Purpose forward. In all relationships, it can be said that wasting oneself where there's no longer a connection or the path has been separated is to wither away in a Soul's prison. To connect with one of your own frequency and makeup is to free the Self to move forward through the halls of destiny.

By honoring your feminine and masculine aspects as equals, you are able to free your Spirit and heal the separation you have endured throughout your known history. It is time to release the old negativity around this separateness and to honor those parts of Self that have been seeking wholeness. This will release the constrictions around your heart, activate your personal power center and remove all fear around receiving love.

Your heart has been hardened by past life traumas and present day memories, but its softening and merging has already begun. Through this process, you are reconnected to the purity and passion of your Soul and granted access to the doorways of Inner Knowing. May you allow the reflection of the love in your Soul to present itself in the person of your twin flame.

Cecelia: *Please give a more complete explanation of the twin flame connection. What does this truly mean?*

Nancy: *It is when the energy of one person is so harmonious in essence, vibration and nature to the energy of another that they cannot help but blend together. It is that similarity, that matched resonance, you long for throughout your life, and even unto the grave if it is not accomplished. There is always a feeling of not quite having what is needed when the connection with the twin flame energy is not found. Many struggles are created in life while looking for this energy. Many disappointments arise out of relationships meant only for the value of their experience. There are many reasons people combine in relationships. All should be valued for the gifts and lessons they bring, but these phantom combinations bear little resemblance to the energy created when you merge with your twin flame. They may leave you with a feeling of emptiness or shallowness, a sense of not having had what was necessary. As soon as the learning experience is completed in ordinary pairings, there is not much left to hold the two Souls together. The twin flame energy, on the other hand, becomes the same as light, breath and water— the most necessary of all elements—once it is* *joined. This relationship has always been and forever will be. When twin flame energies are joined and expressed in the physical, it is the highest degree of companionable interaction. It facilitates the highest levels of joy, love and reconnection to Creator.*

Cecelia: *What happens when twin flame souls create a child?*

Nancy: *There is not one answer to this question. The twin flame energy, when combined, is the most profound coupling possible in the physical. Depending on the life experience and Soul growth of the two humans involved, there are things that may not feel completely comfortable. When the twin flame energy is of a highly evolved nature and the two humans have each recognized the other as their partner, the couple may combine in a way that doubles their own energy.*

The creative channel that allows another Soul to come in through these combined energies is the most joyous passage possible in humanity. The new being arrives as a well-balanced male/female aspect, whether expressing as a male or a female. This being is fully merged within their own physical expression. They do not have to work out the disparity between the energy of two parents who have come together and are relating through disharmonious energy, experience and thinking.

Imagine creating a bridge from two different kinds of building materials, then joining them in the middle. The bridge would be weak at the weight-bearing part of the bridge.

But, if you are driving across a bridge that is made from the energy of love, harmony and combined strength, your passage will be much different.

Cecelia: *Are there any children on the planet currently that are the product of a twin flame union?*

Nancy: *Yes. There are a few.*

Cecelia: *Will they be our leaders in the coming years?*

Nancy: *There is no blanket statement that can be made. Do not expect that to necessarily be the case, although the relationship would create a foundation for the child that* *is more likely to produce such a leader. There are many reasons that beings come into this reality to express their own Inner Knowing and light.*

Many of those who assume positions of leadership are lonely individuals who feel they have no true Home. Others may jump out in front, willing to take risks or to sacrifice all, for there is nothing more that they have interest in achieving. You see, the dynamics of leadership are varied.

The twin flame coupling and the creation of such a child would more likely influence its own family. They would spread the energy of love in their own way, fully connecting spiritually, without having to go out among large groups to create an effect. So you see, this is all subject to the Will, character, disposition and earth life experience of the particular soul.

Cecelia: *Do twin flame energies help one another heal even when they are not together?*

Nancy: *Yes. Absolutely. This is law. The beings closest to that twin flame will receive more of the healing vibration on any issue than those who are connected from a greater distance. For instance, there are friends and family members with whom you share very little actual energetic connection, even if they are physically close. But there are also those, whether near or far, whose compatibility and awareness is so similar to yours that even through a thought form they cannot help but receive. There is a continual energetic exchange between these beings, sharing the joys, the sorrows, the healings and the missteps.*

Normal pairings have a natural and frequent occurrence of energy exchange, especially when a deeper connection has been made through sexual exchanges of energy. When twin flames join in this manner, the vibration of sharing is much more intense. They combine to such a high degree that they are sharing all things in their own frequency. At the time of a twin flame coupling, a bridge is created through which this energy is always running. This coupling creates an energy channel through which they can give and receive, one to the other, at all times. From that point on, they will share everything energetically unless the connection is broken by mutual decision.

Cecelia: *Why are twin flame energies being reconnected at this time?*

Nancy: *There is now the ability to do so. It has to do with the frequency shifts that occur at the ending of one cycle and the beginning of new cycles in man's development. There is a necessity for this dynamic: Heaven cannot be created on earth without the joining of the twin flame energies. This is the next step in grounding this energy into the earth. Until now, the twin flame energy has resembled butterflies fluttering around the planet, flitting to and fro. There has been a sense of longing for something, and—knowing it has not been found among those who are seeking it—a level of connection. And yet, being caught within their own earth experience, they have attempted to search and find this energy in many different ways. All this has been to gather information and add it to that which has already been collected.*

Finding Home was not necessarily first on the experience list of those who came to earth for the physical experience. Does that make sense? As Spirits come to this plane, they are in search-and-curiosity mode and must experience many, many things. As eons have passed and the gathering of experiences has been completed, there is a need to return Home with the one person who can make it possible.

Cecelia: *By returning Home, you are referring to what?*

Nancy: *As above, so below. On earth as it is in Heaven. It means combining physical energy with the power of your Spirit.*

Cecelia: *Will this blending of the twin flame energy create a more powerful network of healing for those who encounter it?*

Nancy: *Absolutely correct.*

Cecelia: *Can you speak more directly about the role intended for these twin flame energies that are working together now?*

Nancy: *When they are truly combined, the twin flame energies spin like a top. The combined energy spins out and through all the areas of the earth—the atmosphere, the universe— gathering information, then returning to share. These energies can return to their place among the Infinite, gathering all resources and bringing them in. The majority of this energy is spent in expansion and in the place of the rejoining with the twin flame. It is a joyous place in which to resonate. Yet, most generously, the twin flame Souls will come down off the mountaintop, into the city and allow the energy of their union to mingle with the masses. They speak the words that allow others to find this place of connection for themselves.*

When they are not speaking or traveling, there will be a tremendous desire for twin flame Souls to withdraw from the world and try to find solace in nature and silence. There is much spiritual strength to be garnered from the gifts of nature—the trees, the waterways and the fresh air that will be breathed. This will be a most joyous interaction from this time forward.

There will also be a need to sever old emotional ties with those with whom they may have had previous intimate relationships. At that point, the couple would have already grieved and released many of the emotional memories they have from the past, but may have needed to sever those bonds and connections on a much deeper level.

There is a need for twin flame Souls to consciously revisit each of their past relationships. Starting from the most recent and moving backward, they need to release those with whom they have had sexual relations, those they have loved deeply, those with whom they have had intense encounters of a high frequency, whether in anger, in love, in joy or in combat. You get the idea. It is not just those they have loved or had physical intimacy with but those with whom they have shared a very intense adrenal response, either in the negative or the positive. Certainly, some have experienced both sides of the coin. In higher-level relationships, they have experienced higher joys as well as more intense areas of conflict.

It is true that you access your deepest level of consciousness with those to whom you have had the deepest attachments. They push all your buttons. These Souls have been part of many of your past lives and participants in your karmic experiences of this lifetime. They have been part of experiences you have buried from conscious memory. They have seen you through other phases of thought, experience and emotion—even those you have felt more comfortable denying or sweeping under the rug. These have been the friends, companions and Spirits who have traveled with you on your journey of Self-discovery. They have helped you look at the uncomfortable pieces of Self—those that have hidden in the darkest tunnels and taken you farthest from the light.

You should tell each of these partners on your journey that you are appreciative and thankful for the many gifts they have given you. Each of them has brought you closer to your new sense of Self. If you think about what we have said, you will know it is certainly true.

It is impossible to stand in the fullness of your own light when another being has attachments to your body, heart and Soul. They can pull and tug in places that are unhealed, which leaves you weakened by the parasitic connection that remains. Many of you have left relationships because of issues that could not be resolved. Though you could not achieve a place of peace in that relationship, you might still long for that person in a meaningful way. If all levels of connection are not in place, those in which you give freely to one another in light and Love, then you are missing out on what was intended for you. We ask you not to judge your previous level of interacting. At the time, it was the best you could do and the best you felt you deserved.

When you open to fully receiving from another, your bond allows you to experience your God Self more fully. This is the beautiful gift of a romantic relationship when it connects on all levels. This great gift from Creator can return you Home while you are still in physical form. It can help you feel the joy, peace and bliss of your connection to Source.

We love you and wish you well on your journey.

Meditation for Release of Past Relationships

Beginning with the individual in your most recent relationship and working backward, we ask you to hold each up in the light so you see nothing but purity and light running through them. The gift of Consciousness and enlightenment you give them also gives you a reflection of who those beings truly are. Seeing those beings washed in the purity of God's light, you can no longer hold onto grudges or areas of darkness or hidden agendas that are beyond the Christed light.

As you hold each of these individuals in the light, repeat the following: "I set free all attachments past, present and future that have been entangled with my energies, now and forever. If future encounters result in these individuals returning to my life, we will have a fresh, new relationship, one with the other, and allow no past deeds to enter into our interactions. Energetically, all ties are severed. There are no hooks, no strings and no bindings that connect us, one to the other. We are one and the same, as the energies of God, and have no particular attachment beyond our light force. In blessing, I do release you."

Chapter Nineteen

YOUR SPIRITUAL FAMILY

The following information, through the combined energy of Mary Magdalene and Jesus the Christed One, was channeled through Nancy.

Nancy: The members of your spiritual family are speaking as one entity. We acknowledge all of you who recognize your partnership with Spirit and have begun to bring yourselves back into union with your Higher Self. We cherish your earth walk.

We have watched closely from the moment of your conception to the present day, and we have seen your joy and your struggle. We do cry for your struggles in the physical flesh, for we recall how that was. Your spiritual family's hope for your Ascension and joyous expansion into the Breath of the One is far more meaningful than you can see while in the physical. You do often hear our whispering and understand there is more to knowledge and awareness than can ever be imagined. The miracle is that you are already in a place of Heaven on earth or Hell on earth—depending upon what you choose to create. You have not yet understood that your life is all about your own creation.

When we see you feeling sorrow for the community of mankind, you feel a core issue in the very essence of your Soul. You are mourning the sadness of the struggle that some will experience as part of their earth walk.

But you are among our emissaries of Divine Guidance. You feel the positive or negative impact of an event instantaneously. You have learned to follow your own Truth. Many unlimited Beings of light speak to you, and you recognize them as higher aspects of your own Being.

We are the ones known to you as Jesus and Mary Magdalene. We are twin flame energies; we have shared many experiences in many lifetimes. We have been in various relationships, one to the other. Many of you resonate with our energies and our combined nurturing love energy. We have been together, learned together and shared our joy and pain together. We have also watched you most closely and encouraged you. Many of you have lived with us—have known us, have been us—and we have been you in our shared experiences.

We will try to give you more understanding about the twin flame energy than was previously discussed. There are many terms that are used in an effort to describe the same thing. There are frequencies and colors aligned with the emotional centers, the intellectual centers and the physical imprinting of the same type of life experiences between twin flame energies. Life stories may be told in different ways or appear to be different stories, but the lessons in the center of each event have been the same—whether in the same or differing lifetimes. There has been a culmination or completion of these lessons, events and histories, whether or not the chronological sequence is in identical order between you and your twin flame. Because of these mutual experiences, you are most resonant with one another. Your twin flame is the being with whom you merge and resonate with most completely. It defines the nature of spiritual marriage. All twin flames are aligned in our realm because they cannot deny those who are their energetic equal. They are your companions throughout many lifetimes, the one energy that is most compatible with your own in the entire universe. This connection cannot be denied in the spirit realm, and yet, it has been completely denied in the physical. The spiritual amnesia caused by the density of the earth has separated many of those who would have done well together had they been able to trust. In the past, this lack of trust and the pain of similar life circumstances created insurmountable emotional and mental blocks. As two Twin Souls longed for individual life experience on the one hand and emotional connection on the other, these two longings were incompatible on most occasions.

Although there is undeniable sexual magnetism in a twin flame partnership, we would also say that twin flames come in other less powerful varieties— mother and child, siblings that are unusually connected and strong friendships. These less powerful connections are called Soul Mates. You are Soul Mated to a number of individual Spirits who combine with you over and over again during many lifetimes for mutual experience.

These beings are all members of your true family. Your earth walk has been about rejoining with those you know on a Soul level. You speak lovingly of them, as we spoke of our own disciples and followers. There are many who lived with us and helped us but were unknown to others in a historical sense. They were not blood connections, yet they were of our same family. When you have that love, joy and connection with others, you recognize them as family on a different level.

To express yourselves from a place of love and peace is the key to continue spreading the love vibration in humanity. You are the same as we are when you are in your expanded state. You cannot be separated from us, even though your physical state has attempted to delude you in that manner. We are here as part of your support team while your earth assignment continues. In addition, many of you are being given additional support and recognition during your reunion with your twin flame.

The joining of twin flame energies is more powerful than either energy could be alone. By joining the strength, intelligence, intuition and experience of the two, they become a stronger, more compatible unit combined with longevity and purpose. This mutual support system is most helpful when one has a spiritual journey to complete.

Several days later, another message on the same subject was channeled through Cecelia.

Cecelia: *As you allow yourselves to open to the voice of Truth that resides within each of you, you begin to be drawn into the company of others who also feel dissatisfaction with the old ways of being. You begin to experience guidance from the higher realms and are less easily deceived about your own true natures. The more guidance you allow in, the more you begin to resonate with the vibration of Divine Love. You are less easily deceived and not as likely to accept people or relationships that take away your energy and inhibit your Soul growth.*

There are many people who are drawn into your lives at the appropriate time in your learning process. They may come in the form of friends, family or intimate relationships. Usually, these are Souls that have been with you in many lifetimes of learning and experience. They may be present to offer you comfort or assistance. They may be here to mirror some unresolved aspect of your personality or essence. They may be here to teach you about yourself. These lessons may not be pleasant, but they are always there for your learning and evaluation of Self.

When you have begun to recognize the value of your own essence and have suspended judgment of others and Self, you feel more peace in your own life. You begin to accept yourself as a Being of light, here to learn and experience physical reality. Eventually, you accept that no one is judging your process but you— that you create your own life situation through your belief system and thoughts. All that is required is for you to do the best you can in the moment, based on your level of growth and spiritual development.

It is a wondrous life when the one most closely attuned to your level of growth and awareness—your twin flame—enters your life experience. It brings with it a sense of peace and a sharing of energy that allows for more positive and powerful creation in your lives. People begin to be drawn to your energy, for they recognize on some level that you have something they connect to in a most satisfying way. They feel energized in your presence, and they can feel your level of commitment, one to the other, free of competition.

Chapter Twenty

TWIN FLAME SEXUALTIY

Nancy and Cecelia jointly opened to receive the following blended messages—this was to serve as an exercise in allowing the sisters to tag team information from one to the other.

We are here to discuss the romance of body, mind and Spirit. We speak of a beautiful harmony and nurturing within the Self, which opens the doorway for a reunion with your twin flame. This reunion is a reuniting of those who are here to serve together. It represents a partnership in which the God Self-energy of one Soul is united with the God Self- energy of another who most closely resonates to their vibration. This high degree of resonance creates powerful partnerships of love to serve as examples to the rest of the planet. It is time for these pairings to be created all around the world. This will allow the maximum effort, energy and power among light Workers. There is perfection to the design of humanity, and it is no accident that the masculine and feminine aspects were designed to work in conjunction with one another, giving and receiving the infinite energy of creation.

The blueprint of the entirety of creation resides within each one of you. The joining of twin flame couples activates this creative blueprint through the divine power of love. This joining represents a return to wholeness within the individual which creates powerful new energy channels. These energy channels can be used to expand this creative force onto the planet. These glorious events signal the impending birth of a new age for the earth and humanity.

We joyfully facilitate the release of this new energy into your keeping. It can be used to activate the healing you have prayed for and grant access to your own unlimited resources. This is the time for the synchronization of the human heart and mind with the pulse of the earth. You can be cleared of past limitations and propelled forward into higher levels of expression. The vibration of Divine love is facilitating all areas of Soul growth and the radiance it creates will be felt throughout the world and beyond.

Eventually all of you will understand how far you have walked and how high you have climbed. You will know and understand that every event, each experience and every encounter in the physical or spiritual realm has been perfect. Even when your soul cried out in anger or pain and begged to be released from what was felt to be too much to endure, you found a way to expand your understanding. Often when you experienced the worst pain, you still learned from the trauma and grew most beautifully. We have seen you overcome so many obstacles and trials and still manage to get up and try one more time. Joyously, we have cheered for you each time you fought your way back and you found a way to fly with success.

Understand that no one has judged how well you have done except yourselves. On some level you have remembered the state of perfection and feared that you would never again obtain that ideal. But we say to you and to all who read these words that there has been perfection in every moment. Even when you have been in the greatest doubt and resistance you were perfectly proceeding toward the next step of your evolution. This steady progression is your life's true purpose and mission. When spirit is fully integrated with mind and body, the physical body and the Self merge into a state of perfection.

When this occurs, you project a sense of confidence, you live in integrity and you are perfectly aligned with your Will, the Will of Creator and the Will of all who are moving toward the Ascension of the planet. As above, so below—on earth as it is in heaven. All is the same at the same time, whether in body or Spirit. Each of you is in a place to merge your Soul with all others. We ask you to never again allow judgment to interfere with your mental or emotional natures. Judgment of Self, judgment of others and judgment of events have acted as a stone about your throat. You do not need to reside in this vibration for one more moment. Release it. Move forward into your place of perfection—into your place of perfection.

As you move into resonance with your twin flame, your individual energies are no longer Self-contained but travel back and forth between the two of you. It is the circling of this energy that creates the dynamic patterns between you. This creates the magnetism that draws others into your field of influence. It is the infinity symbol, or the figure-eight combination of looping energy waves, that creates such power.

When energy travels between twin flames, they are increased in strength and velocity, expanding at a greater rate than possible from one individual. This is why these pairings are so important.

As twin flame Souls integrate the infinity energy flow, wonderful things begin to happen. Long-dormant chakras, sub-chakras and glands begin to function. Their energy quickly activates the new thymus chakra. Through the thymus chakra, you will find yourself being enlivened and regenerated. This will allow both the male and female aspects of yourself and your partner to become balanced and to receive energy in a way once impossible. It is through combining the twin flame energies that you will find the Life Force welling up in you, revitalizing and re-energizing you in a way never known in this lifetime. This dual energy has greater speed, longer range and higher frequency than any other, and it allows higher forms of information to flood into conscious awareness.

Twin Flame Meditation

Get into a comfortable position, and relax. Notice where you are holding tension or constriction in your body, and allow all areas of tightness to leave. Breathe in fully, and picture light entering all areas of your body that are bound tightly. Exhale as you feel the tension leaving. Continue for six breaths.

Turn your attention to Source, and ask to access the feeling of love buried deep within your Soul. This may feel more like a vibration than an emotion. Be still, and allow love to come forward, to rise up within you. Notice that you may begin to feel a slight buzzing or a sensation that feels like champagne bubbles coursing through you. Consciously hold the frequency of the love vibration until it is very strong.

Bring the twin flame vibration into your energy field. Call to you the one being in the universe whose essence is most like yours. Visualize the color pink in joyous union and resonance, surrounding and filling your body; this will invite your twin flame into your life and also awaken a longing in them for your connection, particularly since you resonate on the same level. Recognize what it feels like to be at Home.

Establish a connection between your crown chakra and that of your twin flame. As you focus on the top of your head, picture a white-colored ribbon spinning around it, flowing from your crown chakra to that of your twin flame. Direct this energy to all other chakras and back again in figure-eight form to create the love vibration. Look into the face of your Twin Soul, and, with love, recognize your similarities.

Now envision your third eye chakra opening across your brow, and send the color purple to each other. Envision your beloved's Soul coming to you.

Next, focus your attention on your lips and those of your beloved. Visualize the two of you speaking harmonious words.

Make it your intention that all future communication will come from the heart and the wisdom and compassion of your Souls.

Turn your attention to the throat chakra, and request that the love energy flow into and correct any imbalances. See the blue color of communication swell up and flow through your throat chakra, and release any constriction from your cellular memory. Honor the throat chakra as your place of powerful connection and creation, and share it with your twin flame. The two of you can now speak honestly, openly, lovingly and from the depths of your Souls.

Next, see the energy from your throat chakra extending to the area known as the thymus, right below the throat and just above the heart. When activated, the thymus will help regenerate your physical bodies. Envision the color turquoise, twirling and expanding from the thymus, its rejuvenating properties beginning to activate. Spread this healing energy to the thymus area of your twin flame, knowing that your earthly bodies are becoming younger, and that you have all the energy you both need to heal your bodies and Souls.

Focus now on your heart chakra. Through the energy of love, see the connection to your twin flame, heart to heart, filling your bodies with joy. Release any blocks or constrictions that hold wounds from the past. Ask for the courage to open your heart fully, to keep it open and to use it for internal guidance of the Spirit Within. Make it your intention to release all fear of feeling, and see your heart as fresh, new and healthy. See the color green welling up, spinning and opening the entire chest area. Flow this green energy of love from your heart into the heart of your beloved. Hold this vision until the connection seems complete and you are both filled with love.

Next, focus your attention on the area of the solar plexus, the center of your body located near the ribcage. This is your power center. This location represents how you portray yourself in the world. Allow the color yellow to activate and fill your power center—spinning, flowing outward and reaching the solar plexus of your beloved. See the energy flowing from the one to the other, empowering each with combined strength.

Now, feel the energy of your power center merging with and igniting your creative center, the splenic chakra, in the center of your abdomen. This will re-ignite your creative energy and strengthen your gifts as co-creator. Envision the color orange spinning and filling your abdominal area, opening and expanding your feeling of power in that area. Send this orange energy from your pelvic area to the pelvic area of your twin flame. Allow the energized feeling of procreation to spin out and rush through your bodies.

Finally, turn your attention to your root chakra, which is located at your tailbone, your center of survival and connection to the earth. See the vibrant color red opening up and spinning through the area, penetrating the earth to ground you. Envision this fiery red energy moving into the root chakra of your beloved. Feel the energy pass back and forth between you and your twin flame, grounding, centering and connecting you both to Mother Earth and to each other. This connection will enhance your ability to feel safe in the material world, fortified by your connection to each other and the planet.

You are now ready to physically manifest the joint creations of you and your twin flame in the world. You have connected your Souls through the primary energy centers of the physical body. You should feel that you have come Home to a place of peace, harmony and Oneness. Now, merge your entire essence into the essence of the body and Soul of your beloved. Feel the Oneness. This is the reunion you have longed for. This is the joining of the twin flame energies combined on every level, as occurs naturally beyond the veil.

The feelings of discomfort and sorrow you have experienced are connected to where you feel you were cut off from your feeling of Wholeness. You have longed to feel Whole, guessing that it might happen by connecting you to your other half, your twin flame. That is, indeed, one way. But, opening to your fullness can occur with or without your twin flame present.

This lifetime, many of you have not even come in to be blessed by that union in the physical, but you may nevertheless complete your connection in the manner described in the twin flame meditation. The joining process is non-invasive and allows the acceptance of the love energies as is appropriate. Your desire for these energies have magnetized and attracted them to you.

In relationships where there is lack of interest or connection from one party, there is no resonance. It is not for you to use the twin flame meditation to connect with one who is not of your nature. You should not attempt to create a feeling of connection in a relationship where no connection exists. But, when you respond to a Soul connection, it is mutual. That which you seek seeks you. Your twin flame longs for you as you long for your twin flame.

On some level, your own internal guidance system will lead you to the proper place, time and twin flame when you are ready to be rejoined. This is one of the very best reasons for listening to your Inner Voice—following the dictates of your heart and choosing your activities according to your true nature. When you are drawn to a certain place, and the thought of it makes your heart flutter or expand, realize this is a signal from your Soul. If the notion of a particular place or situation makes you feel flat or energetically low, this, too, is a sign. By listening to your Inner Guidance, you will be led to the right place at the right time to encounter your twin flame.

When you finally connect with your twin flame, you may find that you have shared common lessons in this lifetime. Even though your outer circumstances may appear to be different, the core learning will be much the same. The lessons you have learned and the healing you have been through have affected your twin flame. Much of your timing has been similar. Imagine that the other part of you vibrates to your same frequency. You have magnetized the same lessons for wholeness, one from the masculine perspective and another from the feminine. You have both been on your path to wholeness for hundreds, perhaps thousands, of lifetimes and have shared the same drive and longing to complete the Soul's work and return Home.

But even though the bliss of reconnecting with your beloved is your birthright because you are one with Creator, it may not occur in this lifetime. It may occur as you stand on the other side of the veil.

You must have patience that all things unfold through Divine timing. You may still have lessons to be learned or mental constrictions to be released. You may have an idealized picture of how your twin flame looks and the position they hold in the world. When you have such expectations, you limit the faces of love that may appear as companions, friends or partners on your journey.

By acknowledging that you are exactly where you need to be on your Soul's journey you will experience those things perfect for your learning, feel at ease. Accepting things as they are is integral to honoring your path and continuing your journey. It elevates you on the road to Wholeness, and allows you to make great strides returning Home.

Chapter Twenty-One

THE NATURE OF PERFECTION

Cecelia received the following message to help create an understanding of the correction required in the physical body for it to interact with alternate realms and receive more advanced forms of communication.

Cecelia: *Multiple dimensions have always interpenetrated your world but only recently has this become a significant problem for your physical body. As you try to adapt to the higher frequencies being directed toward your planet you may begin to experience discomfort in various parts of your body. These may present themselves as insomnia or restless legs. Some of you have felt pressure around your head, have experienced more headaches, eye pain, or a sense of a being separate from your world. You may also notice difficulty in concentrating or focusing your attention on the task at hand. Even the weather may create a problem, for it often interpenetrates other dimensions to discharge excess energy.*

The higher frequencies are not always compatible with those who are in a cycle of up-leveling their body and rewiring their energy system. As you accomplish resonance with higher subtle energy you may begin to live with one foot in both worlds at the same time. The over-lapping of these inter-dimensional energies can cause great discomfort until the density of things around you transforms to resonate with your new energy response system.

If it were within our power to make this easier, we would. But this is a process that must be accomplished on the physical level. We cannot assist in lessening your physical discomfort as you go through the cycle of transforming from one energetic expression into another. The process can be shortened in duration, however, if you understand that it is a natural part of your evolution and do not allow yourself to go into anger or resistence over these changes.

We are providing you information about integrating these energies more quickly so it will be less difficult on your body. Our suggestions may appear to be those that have little or no consequence. Yet, if you could see on an energetic level how it affects your entire system, you would not hesitate. This may help you understand why you have been feeling as you do.

In addition, the energies you sense in the middle of the night, when the veil is thinnest between the dimensions, is actually intercommunication and interpenetration between the dimensions. This is the time when higher energies from new dimensional levels and lower energies from your earthly dimension collide, creating discordant energy in your physical system. It may make you feel like you are being shaken from deep within, or it may be associated with heat, muscular twitching and other minor discomforts. Do not be alarmed. This is simply your body attempting to adjust, process and reform itself in its higher energy vibration. Do not fight the energy; allow it to flow. Feel it penetrate your essence, and visualize your body coming into perfect alignment. This will make it easier for you to handle disruptions in your physical body and sleep patterns.

Knowing that you are moving through old patterns should make this process more acceptable. Understand that there is a start and finish to this process. It is subtle in the beginning and in the end, heating up in between. It is like the ebb and flow of the tides and is a natural part of your evolution. Even if you think this sounds unreasonable, know that your time of transformation will occur. It is only a matter of when.

Nancy then received the following channeled message:

Nancy: *Your life circumstances have led you to the present moment. This is the ever-evolving moment of the Now, the only time there is. The events of your life are a reflection of your own responses in times of crisis or change. Now, when you feel burdened or anxious, you are able to flow through it easily. Your life experiences have been for your evolvement rather than your despair, but you have often questioned these experiences. There have been moments when your belief in a Divine Plan has been shaken, when it no longer mattered whether there was purpose to your life, for the pain was too great. Referring to those times, we say, "Blessings to your heart, for you have been too long out of our comfort and care. Open your heart to us again, and we will love you with compassion and understanding. We put our ethereal arms around you and merge with you in love and Holy Grace."*

Many things are changing. Planetary vibrations are multiplying and dividing, moving you into higher dimensions and back again. It is like quickly trying on new garments in a changing closet without checking the mirror to see if the new clothes fit. In such moments, it may be impossible to relate to time or feel centered. During these disorienting shifts, you may find a greater need for quiet time, meditation and grounding to the earth.

As you feel the expansion, contraction and speeding up of events, it may appear that life has clicked on the fast-forward button. The speed at which you are processing information has increased, as have the rates at which you receive images and events. You have begun to open to Cosmic Mind and to the accessibility of All There Is.

Your life experiences have arisen to move you forward. The greatest crises are actually initiations, for these are critical moments of life-changing decisions and acceptance. These are holy moments when you are blessed with a knowing that something has, or must, change, and that you will never again be your former Self.

We wish to acknowledge those of you who are moving diligently along your path. Whatever comes, know that it is a part of what you are co-creating as a necessary part of your evolution. This should give you greater confidence in your choices. There is perfection in all that you are and all that you do.

Chapter Twenty-Two

ASCENSION: BECOMING YOUR FUTURE SELF

Cecelia was the receiver of this final transmission. Listen as the coded messages penetrate your level of Consciousness. Hear what your Soul will allow at this time. Your capacity for Knowing is ever expanding. Open to your future Self.

You have many misconceptions about Ascension. You seem to feel that one day you will simply wake up, a bell will sound and you will be lifted into another world—nothing left behind. But the process of Ascension does not involve leaving this world; it involves remaining here to assist the earth in becoming a finer and brighter place. Ascension involves elevating your vibration, your Consciousness and your thought processes so you can help the earth return to a state of balance.

*This is why it is so important that **you** be in balance. As you balance your own energies, you begin to influence the very air around you. Your system is a high-energy generator. By inhaling oxygen and exhaling its by-products into the air, you release vibrations that are being breathed in by others. Whenever you are in close proximity to another, you breathe*

the same molecules and frequencies and share the same Life essence. This energy exchange causes a chain reaction that can promote higher energy in everyone. It is significant that you understand how important it is with whom you share this very precious space.

We are here to bring those who are ready into their full power. We are here to combine our energy in the name of the One Heart with those who have cleared the way for Ascension. We are ready to activate the One Pulse that is the signal for all other doorways to open.

The One Pulse, the vibrations, will allow the opening into areas of Self that have previously been denied to you. We are multi-colored, spiraling, creative energies of the Eleventh Octave. We reach out to you through time, space and other dimensions to help you embrace your own essence. You are in our direct line of descent and are necessary to the awakening planetary plan of Ascension and the relocation of the physical realm to a higher vibration. The Ascension is not just about humankind or planet earth, or even this universe. There are billions of universes in as many dimensions ready and waiting for the catalyzing effect of the firing of awareness on this physical plane, for it will create countless other firings from the base chakras and grounding energies in all planes of existence. There will be an exponential effect both upward and outward that will move in giant waves of unleashed creative energies.

These energies will be used by all Beings everywhere to begin the re-creation of their lives and their planetary Consciousness. This is, indeed, a time to release unlimited potential into the hands of those who understand right use of Will and carry deep within them knowledge of the Laws of the universe. Those who have shown themselves to be ready to work directly with the planet and Beings from higher vibrational realms are being called into more direct service. There will be a great deal of responsibility given to these expanded Souls, but the rewards will be beyond imagining. The union you have sought through others will now be within you. The love you have sought without will dwell within to help dispel any feelings of doubt or unworthiness. You will feel the love of the Higher Hosts as they shower upon you the gifts of the Unified Being.

You will feel connected to Source. We trust each of you with this heightened sense of energy, for you have shown yourselves to be trustworthy and interested in the betterment of all, without the subjugation of any. You will embody integrity and trust in your interactions.

Keep close to your heart the Universal Responsibility you have, and love those you meet from the place within connected to Divine Love. Live that love, and allow it to shine outward toward all you encounter. Walk in beauty and light, and share generously of yourself. This never-ending source of light and power are available to you at all times; it will never run short.

Our pledge to you is to be available always, to love you always and to make sure you never walk alone. We are your Family in the light, and we are rushing toward you. We are in a process of stepping up your energy to make it easier for you to be in our collective mind. The vibration of your body is slowly being raised to be in attunement with our energy so that we may function with you and through you as a collective energy that will gradually bring your physical vehicle into perfect alignment with our vibration.

Pay attention to your feelings, and heed our promptings as well as your own, for they are the guideposts that will lead you Home.

Chapter Twenty-Three

BLESSING

You are like the rose, perfection in each phase of development. From seedling to stem to bud to bloom, you unfold into the richness of maturity. Even as the bloom fades, each remaining day adds final touches of artistry and beauty to your life expression.

You are as perfect as the rose in every moment. At each level of development, it is both necessary and glorifying to evolve, calling to you the experiences you need to help you proceed.

Even when your Life Force begins to recede, your beauty deepens as it perfumes the air with the essence of rose oil, the most valuable essence on the earth plane because of its unmatched vibrational frequency and purity.

You are like the rose. You are the most precious essence in the world. Like the oil of the rose, you shall remain long after your physical body fades away. You are eternal, your frequency imprinted into the timeless greatness of the One.

When we reflect on our lives and the roads we have traveled, we marvel at how we came to our present existence. We know the importance of opening to Spirit to receive the growth, evolution and understanding of why we are here. In keeping our hearts open to Spirit, penetrating the veil of illusion and accessing unlimited resources, we have chosen to dedicate our lives to our spiritual paths.

We are all recipients of Grace and the unlimited gifts of Spirit if we allow them into our lives. But we must first get beyond our self-limiting beliefs in order to accept that we are powerful, expanded Beings of light residing temporarily in earthly bodies so we can participate in our earth dance.

Had we not healed many of our family wounds through forgiveness and acceptance and had we not allowed the codes of the written teachings to release our past, we would not be where we are today. We are truly grateful to Spirit for walking with us through darkness, with patience and compassion, into receivership of the light.

Embracing our spiritual paths is an ongoing process. When we reach a place of perfection in thought, word and deed, we will be on a higher plane working with loftier issues. We have learned that growth and change are not only possible but necessary in order to make our life experiences both interesting and worthwhile. It is only through doing that we can arrive.

No one can do our work for us. We can expose ourselves to the highest thoughts, the greatest thinkers and the most charitable givers on the planet, but until we act in accordance to our teachings, we are simply treading water. We can complain forever about how badly the world has treated us or we can release the negative charge around the incidents, realize the lessons learned and move forward.

When we find ourselves in similar situations over and over again, it creates a pattern in our lives that may be nudging us to choose differently. It is always our choice whether to change or to stay the same. But no matter what our choices, they always lead us to the same place: Home.

We cannot say how exquisitely special our journey together has been. We have been each other's greatest teacher and dearest friend. We have urged each other to stretch beyond all former boundaries. We have believed in one another when we did not believe in ourselves. We have stood by each other when we felt abandoned, betrayed and utterly alone.

We have done the earth dance together countless times. In past lives together, we have been many races, creeds, colors and religions. We have been male and female. We have been mother, father, brother, sister, child, comrade at arms, master and slave, enemy and friend to each other. In this lifetime, we have come together as sisters to shelter and nourish each other, to encourage each other's growth and to heal our family history.

Our mystical awakening and our connection to unseen worlds might have vanished if we had not been there for each other. We shared our secrets when the world would not listen to, or accept, our gifts. We are blessed by Divine Presence for the gift of our sisterhood.

Many blessings of light to all!

Nancy Lee and Cecelia Keenan

ABOUT THE AUTHORS

Nancy Lee, BA, Honorary DD, is chief executive officer of Visionary Communications, Inc., a multimedia company based in Fort Collins, Colorado, and the author of Voices of Light—Conversations on the New Spirituality published by the Swedenborg Foundation, Chrysalis Books. She is also an internationally known spiritual intuitive, counselor, minister, and speaker.

Lee is the Creator, producer and host of the popular New Thought Radio program, "Lights On with Nancy Lee," heard live since 1997 and on the world wide web through www.nancylee.net and the Healthy Life Network out of Los Angeles, CA, www.healthylife.net.

Lee can be reached at 970-472-9104 or by email at Lee9104@msn.com.

Cecelia Keenan, BA, Honorary DD, is founder and chief executive officer of Energy Recalibration, Inc., an educational counseling organization, and the author of the Energy Recalibration Self-Healing workbook series. A former Speech Pathologist and business owner, she is also a nationally known teacher, speaker and counselor who works with individual clients, businesses and focus groups. She has been a featured speaker at national conferences and a guest on national radio and cablevision shows. Keenan has been a visiting teacher at the world renowned Esalen Institute in Big Sur, California.

Cecelia is a member of the E-Women's Network and National Association of University Women and is listed for 2006 in Empire Who's Who of American Business Women.

She can be reached at 970-495-4804 or by email at ceil49keenan@comcast.net.

Printed in the United States
57996LVS00005B/448-474

9 781425 922566